You Have
Control!

Being a Better Flying Instructor

You Have Control!

Being a Better Flying Instructor

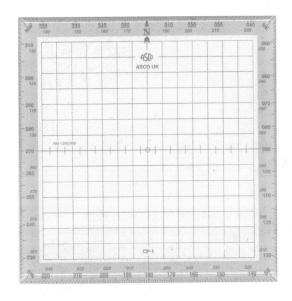

Claire Louise Hatton

The Crowood Press

First published in 2006 by
The Crowood Press Ltd
Ramsbury, Marlborough
Wiltshire SN8 2HR

www.crowood.com

British Library Cataloguing-in-Publication Data
A catalogue record for this book is available from the British
Library.

ISBN   1 86126 818 1
EAN   978 1 86126 818 1

Dedication
For Martin and Thomas

Acknowledgements
I could not have written this book without the endless
support, encouragement and assistance of my husband Martin,
and my parents, Hilary and Walter Davison. I must also thank
my son, Thomas Joseph, who was a mere bump throughout
nine months of the writing process, but whose imminent
arrival towards the end spurred me on to completing it.

I would also like to thank Ian Buchan, John Patterson and
Manchester School of Flying, whose aircraft appear in the
photographs. It was here that I gained my first experience in
aviation, as a fourteen-year-old schoolgirl with an ambition to
become a pilot, and seven years later my first job as a flying
instructor.

Typeset by NBS Publications, Basingstoke, England
Printed and bound in Great Britain by Biddles Ltd, King's Lynn

CONTENTS

LIST OF ABBREVIATIONS

AIC	Aeronautical Information Circular
AIP	Aeronautical Information Publication
AIS	Aeronautical Information Service
AME	Aviation Medical Examiner
ATC	Air Traffic Control
ATPL	Airline Transport Pilot's Licence
ATZ	Aerodrome Traffic Zone
BECMG	Becoming (in a TAF)
C of G	Centre of Gravity
CAA	Civil Aviation Authority
CFI	Chief Flying Instructor
CPL	Commercial Pilot's Licence
DH/MDH	Decision Height/Minimum Descent Height
DOC	Designated Operational Coverage
DV	Direct Vision
ETA	Estimated Time of Arrival
FIS	Flight Information Service
FREDA	Fuel, Radio, Engine, Direction, Altimeter
ILS	Instrument Landing System
IMC	Instrument Meteorological Conditions
IR	Instrument Rating
JAR	Joint Aviation Requirements
JAR-FCL	Joint Aviation Requirements Flight Crew Licensing
MATZ	Military Air Traffic Zone
NOTAM	Notices to Airmen
NPPL	National Private Pilot's Licence
Ops	Operations
PFL	Practise Forced Landing
plog	pilot's log
PPL	Private Pilot's Licence
PPR	Prior Permission Required
PROB	Probability (in a TAF)
PTT	Push To Talk
R/T	Radio Telephony
RIS	Radar Information Service
TAF	Terminal Area Forecast
TDA	Temporary Danger Area
TEMPO	Temporarily (in a TAF)
TRA	Temporary Restricted Area
VFR	Visual Flight Rules
Z	ZULU (Greenwich Mean Time)

INTRODUCTION

When someone qualifies as a flying instructor it is a great achievement. They have proved their ability to pass all the theoretical knowledge examinations for the Commercial Pilot's Licence and have demonstrated a very high standard of flying in order to complete and pass the commercial flight training course and Skill Test. Throughout the Flight Instructor Course they will have gone on to revise the theory behind each flight exercise in the form of long and short briefings, and will have learnt how to teach each specific lesson in the air. Does this prepare them for all that the actual job entails, however? I personally believe the answer to this question is 'no'.

The intention of this book is therefore to provide some additional information to the newly qualified flying instructor, or pilots training towards this qualification.

The majority of these instructors will initially be involved in teaching students training for the PPL or NPPL, although much of the content of the book applies equally to those instructors teaching additional ratings and advanced flying qualifications such as the IMC, CPL or IR. It applies to instructors working in any type of flying school or club environment, as these in themselves can vary enormously; most flying schools and clubs employ ops staff to carry out certain tasks and ensure the smooth running of the daily flying programme, but in other circumstances the instructor may be operating completely alone and will therefore have to do everything for themselves. Whatever the situation, each school will be operating in accordance with the same fundamental CAA rules but will also have their own rules, regulations and methods of operation, which again can be decided upon in a variety of ways, be it an individual owner ultimately making the decisions, or an entire committee.

There is also the input of the CFI to take into account. The CFI at a flying school or club will set down specific guidelines for the instructional staff to work by, but in terms of the day-to-day job, some CFIs have a significant influence on how their instructors operate whilst others prefer to leave the instructors largely to their own devices.

The book is in no way a repeat of the Flight Instructor Course, as it does not tell an instructor what to teach his or her students. In fact there is very little mention of the details and content of specific ground and airborne exercises that are taught during a student pilot's training as, in practice, the actual lessons delivered to each student only form a small part of a flying instructor's day. Instead, it offers general guidance in other areas of the job and things to think about that may not otherwise present themselves until a particular situation arises.

In flying there is often a variety of methods available to carry out the same task, and your approach to teaching will largely be influenced by the way you were taught yourself; in addition to this you will inevitably be given advice by your fellow instructors when you start work at a flying school. When I first started work as an instructor there were many occasions when I went about things as I saw fit, and then afterwards realized how I could have done them a lot better. When you are setting out as a new instructor it is invaluable to listen to the experiences of others, whether these experiences are good or bad, and whether you consider the advice to be useful or not. I can only write from my own experience, about things that have happened to me and to other instructors I know: therefore the content of this book should not be taken as definitive, rather as an additional source of information and advice.

Note on the Text

Throughout this book, I have used the term 'flying instructor' rather than 'flight instructor', except where the actual Flight Instructor Course is referred to. I have also used the term 'weight and balance' rather than 'mass and balance'.

It should be noted that this book is not an authoritative source of documentation or information. It does not in any way overrule, replace or supersede the Air Navigation Order, Aeronautical Information Service, Joint Aviation Requirements, Aircraft Flight Manual, Pilot's Operating Handbook, Flying Order Book, training syllabus, or any other authoritative documents. Nothing in this material overrides any rules, regulations or procedures laid down by the Civil Aviation Authority, Joint Aviation Authorities or aircraft manufacturers.

CHAPTER 1
PROFESSIONALISM

'Professionalism' is an all-encompassing term that is really just a reflection of what you say, what you do and how you do it. In order to become a flying instructor you already need to be the holder of a professional pilot's licence, and therefore when working as a flying instructor you are working as a professional pilot. It is a fact that a large proportion of people who become flying instructors only do so for one reason, as a stepping-stone towards flying for the airlines, but for the time that they are working as instructors they are professional pilots. Your students are paying a huge amount of money for their flying lessons, and as their instructor you are personally responsible for ensuring that they receive the best possible tuition. You must make the most of every flight when deciding where to go and exactly what to do, to ensure their safety and enjoyment, and value for money.

Above all there will be times when you will have sole responsibility for your students' lives. Think about sending a student on their very first solo flight. How many people, during the course of an average day at work, have to accept anywhere near that level of responsibility? The answer is, very few. Whether you are intending to instruct as a route to the airlines, as a career in itself, or just as a hobby, you must accept that it is a very responsible job and you must act as professionally as you can both on the ground and in the air. Flying is great fun and your students should enjoy every flying lesson they have, or there is little point. However, when you are the instructor you must maintain a high level of professionalism at all times. You must ensure that your lessons are conducted thoroughly and safely, and work towards the ultimate aim of instilling the importance of these values into the next generation of qualified pilots.

HAVING A PROFESSIONAL ATTITUDE

A professional attitude to your work starts with being reliable. Each flying school will have its own rules about their instructors' attendance at work, such as whether they should arrive at work at a certain time every day, regardless of their bookings and the weather, or whether they should only come in when they are due to fly. This will largely depend upon whether the school pays them a salary, or whether they are only paid for the actual flying that they do. Some instructors will be available to fly every day and others on a part-time basis, either to fit around other jobs or as a hobby. It is essential that, whatever situation applies to you, you do arrive at work on the days and at the times that you are expected.

The instructor's uniform is generally a white shirt, black trousers and company tie.

If your attendance at the flying school is to be anything other than regular, a diary is necessary in order to keep track of the days and times that you have booked yourself in to fly, particularly if you have booked yourself in several weeks in advance. If you have said that you are available to fly on a particular day and have put your name in the booking sheets, it is likely that the ops staff will have booked some flying in for you on that day. I have witnessed occasions where instructors have booked themselves in but then forgotten all about it, failing to arrive at the school when both the ops staff and their students were waiting for them. Reliability is essential to your colleagues and your customers alike, so if you ensure that you are always there when you say you will be, everyone can benefit.

Having a professional attitude to your job inevitably includes being conscious about your appearance. It may in reality be superficial, but it is a fact that you must look professional in order convey a professional image of both yourself and your workplace; as ridiculous as it is, someone arriving for a flying lesson will have far more confidence and feel much safer in the hands of somebody who 'looks like a pilot'. Most flying instructors will be given detailed instructions from their flying school about what they should, and should not, wear to work, and this normally consists of a white or blue (ironed!) shirt, a company tie and smart black or navy trousers (whether male or female) with a company sweat-shirt or NATO-style jumper, smart clean shoes and possibly a company flying jacket.

In addition to your actual clothing, it is also preferable to arrive at work not only with clean teeth, but with fresh breath. When you consider that your job involves one-to-one briefings with the students, often in a very small classroom, followed by an hour or more in the confines of a very small cockpit, it will be a wholly unpleasant experience for them if your breath reeks of garlic from the night before. It is difficult to avoid eating garlic and other offending foods all the time, but you should try to keep their consumption to a minimum when you know that you are due to fly early the next morning, before it has had time to wear off. Alternatively, or additionally, use a strong mouthwash to neutralize any smells as much as possible. Not only will your students be eternally grateful but you will feel less self-conscious about breathing on people, too.

Acting in a Professional Manner

A professional attitude does not only concern having clean shoes, fresh breath and arriving at work on time, however: it also includes your overall conduct from the moment you arrive at the airfield. After all, it will not impress your first booking of the day, a nervous trial lesson customer, if they watch you walking across the car park in an un-ironed shirt whilst simultaneously trying to tie your tie and comb your hair with your fingers before you reach the front door – and nor will it impress your boss! Good personal organization is an essential part of having a professional attitude, being thoroughly prepared and arriving at work completely ready to start the day.

Part of this organization and preparation should be eating a good breakfast before you set off from home so that you are physically and mentally prepared for the day ahead and not distracted by hunger. Many working people, through lack of time or inclination, skip breakfast altogether and will instead choose to eat something at their desk, or wait until their mid-morning break for something to eat. As a flying instructor, however, you are in a very different situation: it is one thing to sit at a desk all morning having not eaten, but an altogether different experience to go flying a light aircraft, with its associated bumps and bounces, on an empty stomach. Even those with a cast-iron constitution are likely to feel pretty dreadful, and will undoubtedly have difficulty in concentrating and delivering a worthwhile lesson to their students. You can also not afford to be hungry when you might have to make split-second decisions or deal with an emergency.

Flying instructors will rarely have the luxury of a 'mid-morning break' at a specific time, so are unlikely to be able to rely on this as an opportunity to eat. Whether you were previously a breakfast person or not, therefore, eating breakfast before you leave home every morning is really a necessity when you are a flying instructor.

For the same reason, it is also vitally important that you bring food with you to eat during the day, whether it is something you have brought from home or bought from a shop on the way into work. Flying schools vary tremendously in their availability of what might be called 'proper' food, ranging from full restaurant facilities to a snack machine full of chocolate, which may or may not actually work. They are also often located at airfields where the nearest place to buy food is a car journey away. If you have a very busy day ahead, it is extremely unlikely that you will have time to drive to a petrol station or shop to buy some lunch.

If your school does have a restaurant or café, the days on which they are busiest are likely to be the same days that you are busiest – when the weather is good and everyone is flying. On these busy days it is unlikely that you would have time to wait for a meal to be cooked, because if you are busy then the restaurant or café is also likely to be busy. In such circumstances, you will be left with the option of chocolate for lunch, at best, or at worst nothing at all. This is an unacceptable position to put yourself in because there is no way you can fly all day with nothing substantial (i.e. at least a sandwich) to eat. You must therefore make sure that you are sufficiently organized to bring food in with you so that you don't then have to worry about it.

On the subject of professionalism where food is concerned, having gone to the trouble of bringing sandwiches into work, it does not then give a good impression if you take them flying with you! You will see in Chapters 2 and 7 that there will be many occasions when you will have very little time to eat your lunch during a busy day, but you must still ensure that you do eat, and you should try whenever possible do so during your few moments on the ground, rather than when you are airborne. Apart from the fact that you are likely to get whatever it is all over yourself and the aircraft, a light aircraft cockpit is a very confined space and the last thing your student will want is to be subjected to the aroma of your tuna sandwiches. Not at all pleasant for anyone, especially when they are trying to concentrate. If you are setting off on a navigation trip and don't have the chance to eat before you go, take your lunch with you to eat downroute by all means, but try not to eat in the air – unless you are absolutely desperate!

A final thought on acting in a professional manner. As a professional pilot you should be able to recognize when you are unfit to fly and, if so, recognize the importance of staying away from the flying school. We all know deep down when we are fit to fly and when we're not, and there really is no point in going into work just pretending that you are well enough, particularly if you are contagious. For example, there is nothing more annoying for instructors who earn their money solely from flying when someone comes into the school with a cold that they are all likely to catch – worse still if that person is a fellow instructor who should know better. If you are ill, let ops know straight away so that they can try to make alternative arrangements for your students, but even if they can't there is nothing you can do about it. Make your apologies, then stay at home and get better.

CAPTAINCY

Being professional about your job, appearance, and general conduct is important, but the main area where professionalism is so vitally important is in terms of you as the captain of your aircraft. You must thoroughly carry out your duties as the captain of your aircraft not only in order to maintain a professional image for yourself, but also to uphold and promote the professional image of your flying school. Your actions as a flying instructor are representative of the school you are working for, so will directly reflect upon the school and therefore upon everyone else who works there. You should also be setting an example for your students to learn from, and hopefully follow, as aircraft captains themselves.

Documents and Paperwork

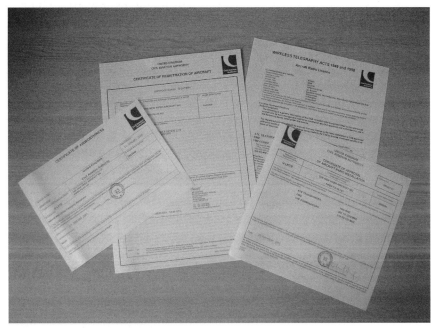

You must ensure that all aircraft documents are valid.

There are many things that ops generally have responsibility for but which are ultimately your responsibility when acting as captain of the aircraft, such as keeping track of the validity of each aircraft's documents. It is therefore personally up to you to ensure that everything is in order before you go flying. You must also ensure that you complete the aircraft tech log before every flight, checking that any ongoing defects are acceptable (if in doubt, ask an engineer), that any work carried out has been correctly signed off and that the aircraft has sufficient hours remaining for your flight to go ahead.

After every flight you must fill in the flight details, including a note of any defects and any oil put in – the oil will be noted either in a column on the tech log or on a separate oil log. Making a note of the quantity of oil put into the engine is often neglected but is in fact very important, as this information can sometimes give an early indication of potential engine problems. It is also your responsibility to ensure that every time you fly you adhere to all weight and balance limitations and cross-wind limitations: if you were to have an incident where any of these were found to have been exceeded, the insurance policy would be invalid.

You must also ensure that you always take off with sufficient fuel for your proposed flight, plus contingencies. This seems too obvious to even mention, but I have witnessed an occasion when an aircraft was being refuelled and the amount of fuel it took was very nearly its entire fuel capacity, meaning that it must have been virtually empty when it landed – and the last person to fly it had been an instructor with a student. I do not need to highlight the severity of this situation because it so clearly could have ended in disaster (as not all forced landings are successful) and you would be unlikely to find work as a professional pilot in the future if it was known that you had made a forced landing simply because you ran out of fuel – this in addition to the highly likely outcome of being prosecuted by the CAA! The repercussions of running out of fuel due to negligence are too awful to even contemplate, but if you are thorough and act professionally this particular problem should never affect you.

It is also essential that you fly with the current aeronautical chart for every area that you may find yourself over and that you check the NOTAMs every day so that you are informed of any airfield, ATC or airspace restrictions. Failure to do so could result in an embarrassing situation if you did something that you shouldn't have done or flew somewhere that you shouldn't have flown, purely because your chart was out of date or because you had not read something that was on the NOTAMs. As a professional pilot there are no excuses for slackness!

In terms of documents and paperwork, another very important item is your school's Flying Order Book (FOB). When you first start work as an instructor you should be handed the FOB to read and digest, and then sign to say that you have done so. It contains all the flying school's operational rules and regulations, with updates and amendments to these as and when they occur. Much of the content of the FOB is very relevant to your day-to-day flying, so it is vital to make a mental (or physical) note of specific details, such as cloudbase and visibility minima for solo navigation, so that you can refer to them when necessary. It is your responsibility to ensure that you are operating in line with your school's specific rules at all times.

Weather

You must always ensure that you have obtained the very latest weather information and use this to make a sensible decision on the suitability of the weather for your lessons. Sometimes the weather will be forecast to be perfect all day with clear sky, good visibility and little wind, whereas at other times the forecast will be dreadful with very low cloud, poor visibility and a gale blowing straight across the runway. Each of these scenarios has its merits as they are both completely unambiguous in terms of the decision you will make (definitely flyable for all lessons, or definitely not flyable for any lessons!). There are many occasions, however, when the decision is not so easy to make because the forecast may include BECMGs, PROBs or TEMPOs, or the weather may appear not to be actually doing what the forecast says it should be doing.

The main priority where the weather is concerned is to ensure that you always access the most current information available at that time. By doing this, you are giving yourself the best chance of the information being accurate and therefore the best chance of the decisions you base upon it being good ones. (*See* Useful Information for details of TAF issue times.) Generally speaking, the forecasts become more accurate as the day progresses, so if you can afford to make a decision later – based on the later forecast – then the more accurate the information is likely to be. For example, if your three o'clock student telephones the flying school at nine o'clock in the morning to check the weather for his lesson, it would be advisable to ask him to call back later in the day when the later forecasts are available (the 1019 TAF or, ideally, the 1322 TAF) just to be sure.

It is a sad fact that some instructors insist on taking their students flying when the weather conditions are obviously not suitable, purely because the instructor wants the flying hours. It is undoubtedly frustrating when the weather prevents your lessons from going ahead, but there is absolutely nothing you can do about it and you have to just accept it as being part of the job. Even students who are right at the beginning of their flying course can recognize when they are being taken advantage of, because they come back from their lessons having learned nothing and probably having had a thoroughly miserable time (as one does, flying around in a light aircraft in bad weather!).

Flying schools can quickly earn themselves a very poor reputation in this respect, even if only one of their instructors is really the culprit, and they will eventually pay the price as their students will just leave to continue their training elsewhere. Everyone can be genuinely caught out by unpredicted weather conditions from time to time, but if this does happen, explain to your student that the weather is not what was forecast and therefore you are having to return to the airfield – never be tempted to 'press on'. They may be disappointed but will understand, and if it is clear that you are doing your best to give your students the most from their lessons then they are more likely to stay loyal to you in return.

Winter Operations

On the subject of weather, it is imperative that during the winter months you are very conscious of ice, both on the ground and in the air. Trying to de-ice

Aircraft must be thoroughly de-iced before flight.

frozen aeroplanes is one of the most miserable jobs going, but it must be done, and done thoroughly, before you can even think about getting airborne. Even if your aircraft live in a cosy hangar they will still be at risk of icing up as soon as they are pulled out if it is cold enough, and you cannot fly with any ice on the airframe whatsoever. It is essential for yourself and your students to wrap up warm on days such as these, as you still want to make sure that all the pre-flight checks are carried out thoroughly, and not rushed because people are cold.

Exercise extreme caution when taxiing on aprons and taxiways; at small airfields there will often be areas that are not de-iced at all, and even at large airports there may be areas that are not completely de-iced, or have re-frozen. Also bear in mind the extra minutes that you will need for the engine to warm up sufficiently for carrying out the power checks, and whilst you are sitting at the hold for this extra time, keep an eye on the airframe for ice forming again. If ice is starting to appear, you must return to the apron for more de-icing. Once you are airborne, make regular visual checks of your airframe to make sure that no ice is forming. Studying the Metform 214 thoroughly before you go will show you the level of the 0°C isotherm, but as with any forecast it is only a prediction, so be vigilant at all levels just in case.

Situational Awareness and Judgement
Throughout each and every flight you must work hard to maintain good situational awareness. Previously, you would have been able to concentrate on handling the aircraft, navigating and talking to ATC, with only perhaps

the distraction of a passenger to deal with. Now, as an instructor, you must be able to do all these things whilst at the same time teaching somebody to fly. The ability to keep one eye (and one ear) on what is happening outside the cockpit is essential for an instructor because you must be constantly monitoring where you are, keeping a good lookout for other traffic and liaising with ATC, in addition to conducting your lesson.

You must be maintaining a listening watch for the position of other aircraft, and what they are doing, just as you would on any other flight, and be vigilant for any other information that may affect you such as a TDA or TRA being established in your vicinity. You must also keep the time at the forefront of your mind, because you do not want to finish your lesson and then realize that you are twenty minutes away from the airfield – resulting in your student having to pay for an unnecessary twenty minutes' flying time and you being late for your next lesson. You should judge it so that you complete the lesson in a suitable position for rejoining, thereby maintaining a slick and professional operation.

Your judgement will also be tested throughout each lesson that you give, whether it is a student's first lesson or their final lesson before their Skill Test. You need to have the confidence to let the student take control, and for as much of the time as possible; if you are constantly all over the controls, your student will never have the confidence to believe that they are doing it themselves. Equally, however, you must be able to judge when to take control back from them. During lessons conducted at altitude this is not usually urgent, with the possible exception of a badly executed stall recovery (and imminent spin). Any exercise that involves the ground at close proximity, however, is going to demand a greater degree of urgency if it all goes wrong, and you should be permanently on standby for it all going wrong, at any moment.

There is an extremely fine balance between allowing the student to maintain control of the aircraft for as long as possible, and intervening before they do anything that would compromise safety. You must allow them to fly the aircraft, because they will never learn how to land if you jump in and take control from them every time (as much as you might like to!), but in so doing it is inevitable that they will make mistakes. Your job is just to recover the situation immediately whenever you feel it is necessary.

More generally, it is also essential that you never allow the student to put yourselves and the aircraft in an uncomfortable or potentially dangerous situation, such as a PFL that is clearly not going to work. This is a perfect example because many an engine failure has occurred during PFL training, where the instructor applies full power to climb away and finds that there is no power there (resulting in the 'PFL' becoming a real 'FL'). You will often see that a student's attempt at a PFL is not going to work long before they do, and whilst you do need to let them see this for themselves so that they can learn from it, you must always have an escape plan – look for and keep in mind another field that you could land in for real, if necessary. If it is clear

Always check the aircraft yourself.

that the student is aiming to 'land' too long or too short for their field, or if you can see that their choice of field is unsuitable (with no other good options), do not leave it until you are at 500ft, just to prove a point: go around in plenty of time.

Sending a student on their first solo flight (or indeed any subsequent solo flight) is when your judgement is really tested. As their instructor you do have a duty of care for your student's safety, but at the same time, solo flying forms an integral part of the flying course. If they are flying to a consistently high standard and making sensible decisions, then you have got to let them go.

Only Rely on Yourself

In your day-to-day job you will be working alongside other pilots, instructors and students at various stages of their training, and inevitably there will be times when you help each other out. As an instructor, however, the responsibility for the safety of your aircraft and its occupants lies completely with you, whatever someone else may do for you: from checking the weather to fuel-draining the aircraft, and no matter how experienced they are, remember that you can only truly rely on yourself and nobody else. This is particularly relevant to someone doing the walkround checks on an aircraft that you are about to fly: regardless of how many times they have checked the aircraft out before, whether they have a licence or are even a fellow instructor, you should not be satisfied until you have checked it out for yourself. Accepting someone else's word that the aircraft has enough fuel or oil for your flight is not sufficient, and it may be that they have missed something that is wrong with the aircraft, or were happy with something that you would not have been happy with yourself.

Another situation in which you cannot simply rely on other people is where a student has previously been sent solo by another instructor and you are due to send them for some more solo work. It is entirely up to you to check that they have the relevant paperwork in place for this to go ahead, such as a current medical certificate and passes in the written exams as specified by your flying school. It might seem reasonable to assume that if the student has flown solo on a previous occasion then they must already have the necessary paperwork in place, but this is not always the case. It may be that they have been learning to fly over a long period of time and that their medical certificate or exam passes – or both – have now expired.

It is also possible that they never actually had them in the first place. I do know of a conversation between an instructor and a student who had just completed his third hour of solo circuit consolidation, which involved the instructor asking for the student's medical certificate to photocopy, and the student replying 'What medical?'. If a student is flying solo under your supervision then you are responsible for ensuring that they are doing so legally. Luckily he wasn't, but if this student had been involved in some sort of incident whilst flying solo, it would have been his instructor who got into serious trouble. Never assume, always check.

INTERACTIONS WITH COLLEAGUES

As a professional pilot it is important to be able to interact effectively and have good working relationships with your colleagues. At any flying school the engineers, ops staff and instructors are ultimately working towards the same common goal: to keep as many aircraft in the air for as long a time as possible. There is really only one way to successfully achieve this, and that is by trying to be sympathetic and understanding of each other's problems in order to work together as a whole body. It is inevitable that there will occasionally be conflicts or disagreements in the workplace, but in general no single party can afford to work against another by being awkward or by making unreasonable demands as this will generate bad feeling, a situation which is not at all conducive to a happy and effective working environment.

I have come across situations in flying schools where there have been problems of this nature and, unfortunately, the single party who is to blame is often the instructor. An instructor might annoy ops by taking someone else's aircraft and disrupting the flying programme, or they may upset the engineers by storming into the hangar demanding to know why their aircraft is not ready. We all know how irritating it can be when someone acts unreasonably, especially if their actions have an effect on us, or if in doing so they are accusing us of something, be it directly or indirectly. To develop and then build on good working relationships with your colleagues, therefore, you must deal with all situations in a professional manner.

To use the two examples above, it may be that the instructor suddenly realized that the aircraft he was booked to fly in did not have the kit that he needed for his lesson, so he had to take a different one, even though another instructor was about to take it. To avoid the confusion and subsequent disruption, it would have been better to very quickly explain the situation to ops who could have passed the message on, with apologies, to the other instructor. In the second example, instead of storming into the hangar and accosting the engineers, the instructor could have calmly and quietly asked if they had an idea of how much longer the aircraft was likely to be, to enable him to make his plans accordingly.

Unexpected, difficult or awkward situations will occur every day, but to deal with them effectively you should involve thought, understanding and, where necessary, a little bit of compromise. Often, issues can arise to do with certain tasks being carried out in and around the flying school, such as who has the responsibility of moving aircraft around the apron, putting on the aircraft covers or tying the aircraft down. Sometimes ops are expected to do these jobs and sometimes the pilots themselves will be expected to do them. Occasionally there will be legal or insurance reasons why only certain people can do certain tasks but most things can be done by anyone, so common sense should be used as much as possible in order for people to get on with their day – and hence everyone can benefit.

Refusing to move an aircraft that is blocking you in because it is supposed to be an 'ops job' is not doing anybody any favours, and will just get on people's nerves. Equally, leaving your aircraft deserted in the middle of the apron is obviously going to cause problems for everybody else, so it is easier all round just to push it out of the way yourself. Professionalism in this sense is just a demonstration of common sense and good airmanship, whether it is helping out by doing something that is not officially 'your job' or by taking the initiative to move another pilot's abandoned chocks from the middle of the apron.

Another small but very important point on maintaining peace and harmony with your colleagues is to always check, and check again, that you are not about to go home with the aircraft keys in your pocket. It is all too easy to do and causes chaos for everyone else the next day if it happens to be your day off and you are not there, but is also easy to avoid – so do your best to avoid it!

In your dealings with ATC you should always be calm and professional, as they too are your colleagues in the wider sense. ATC will always be doing their best and it is no use getting annoyed and impatient with them if it appears that they are ignoring you, because they won't be. On one occasion I was at the hold with two other light aircraft, having been there for a few minutes during a particularly busy period, when one of the pilots called ATC to ask, in a clearly confrontational voice, if we were going to be held there very much longer. ATC were obviously extremely busy, doing their utmost to get everyone away with as little delay as possible, and there really had been no gaps whatsoever in which we could have taken off so far. (I wouldn't have blamed them for holding us there even longer, just to teach the pilot a lesson!) It was very unprofessional of this pilot (also an instructor, who should have known better) and it portrayed a very bad image of us as a whole, as we were all from the same flying school.

Communication

Many of the problems arising at flying schools are a direct result of poor communication. You need to keep ops informed of what you are doing throughout the day so that they can keep track of where you are up to on your flying programme, when you will need fuel, when you will need booking in for circuits, and so on. It will help to keep everyone's day running as efficiently and productively as possible.

Good communication also applies to any problems that you may encounter as you work through your flying programme, such as the weather deteriorating in a particular area or a technical problem with your aircraft. It is important to mention the weather because ops can then pass this information on to other instructors and pilots who might have been planning to head in that direction, and it is imperative to report a technical problem – however small – so that the engineers can be contacted to minimize any disruptions to the flying programme later on. Obviously, if you have had a significant technical problem then ops will know about it anyway because you will be back early, perhaps having not even taken off at all, or perhaps followed by the fire services! It is the minor problems, those that you can easily forget to mention, which can cause real problems later on.

I was once on a trial lesson, flying along quite happily, when the back of my seat suddenly collapsed. The tiny bolt keeping it upright had sheared off, so I was left having to sit as if on a stool with the back of my seat near horizontal. Luckily the person I was with had done a little bit of flying before and worked at the airport, so was not at all fazed by this rather comical situation. As we made our way back towards the airfield I soon adapted to my new seating position, and within a few minutes it was as if nothing had happened. Eventually we landed, taxied in and parked up. I signed his trial lesson certificate and he went home. This was my last flight on a busy Sunday so, having pottered around inside the flying school for a while writing up my day's student records, gathering my belongings together, and so on, I went back out on to the apron, tied the aircraft down, put its cover on and went home.

The next few days had very poor weather, and later in the week when we did fly, this specific aircraft did not happen to be used. It was only on the Saturday – nearly a week since I had flown it – when the problem emerged. A

PPL holder had gone outside to check it out, and came straight back in again saying that he couldn't fly it because the seat was broken. Indeed it was – I had completely forgotten to mention it to anybody, so the aircraft had been sitting in the corner all week with ample opportunity for it to be fixed, but nobody had fixed it because nobody knew it was broken!

In my defence, I had written the problem in the 'defects' column of the tech log, but because the aircraft had not been used and, coincidentally, ops had not had any reason to look in the tech log all week, my entry had remained unread. As it turned out I was actually lucky, because although this occurred at the start of a busy weekend the engineers did manage to fix it very quickly, so the day's flights were not delayed by much at all. However, if they had not been able to fix it there would have been chaos as, with everything else already fully booked, all the bookings for that aircraft would have had to be cancelled for the entire weekend!

The lesson to be learned from this story is that whenever you have a technical problem, always tell ops when you return so that they can deal with it straight away. To help you remember to do this, make a note of it on your kneeboard, somewhere that you can't possibly miss it. The worst culprit for this is discovering during your walkround that a navigation light or landing light is not working. If you are flying in the daytime this is not much of a problem, and by the time you return from your flight you will probably have forgotten all about it. It is a big problem, however, to the instructor who was meant to be flying your aircraft that evening after dark: if it had been reported during the day it could have been fixed in ten minutes, but all the engineers with the spare bulbs will have gone home by the time the other instructor re-discovers the problem – so no navigation light means no night flying for your poor colleague.

Ever since my 'seat experience', if I now have a technical problem I make a note on my kneeboard to remind me when I land, I verbally tell ops and leave a big note on their desk, and I leave the aircraft's tech log open on the relevant page, also on their desk: I want to make sure that I have everything covered and that I have well and truly done my bit to get the problem sorted out!

On another communication issue, if you are planning to visit another airfield during your flight, telephone them to say that you are coming. As already discussed, Air Traffic Units and staff at other airfields are our colleagues in the wider sense, and the more information we can give them about where we are and what we are doing, the better. This applies irrespective of whether an airfield is stated as PPR being mandatory or not, and is purely an extra safety measure. To highlight the importance of this, I will use an example that could have been truly disastrous, had it not been for one very small coincidence.

On the day in question the weather was absolutely hideous, with rain, very low cloud and very poor visibility – a really nasty winter day. I was working at an airfield located very close to a range of mountains that was totally invisible on that particular day due to the thick cloud, and myself and the other instructors were drinking tea, resigned to the fact that we were not going to get any flying done whatsoever. A man arrived at the airfield and sat down with a cup of coffee, looking out of the window. After a few minutes he came over to us and asked if we had heard from an aircraft that had been due in half an hour earlier, because his friend was meant to be flying in. We said that nobody would be coming in with the weather as it was, but we went up to the tower just to check if anyone had telephoned to PPR (mandatory at our airfield), or had called up on the radio, which they had not.

Shortly after this there was a telephone call from the police, again asking if any aircraft had been due into our airfield, because some walkers in the mountains had reported what they thought was the sound of a light aircraft followed by a loud bang. Just to rule out the possibility, we telephoned the airfield that the man said his friend had been coming from, to check whether any of their aircraft had indeed set off bound for our airfield. To our horror they said yes, an aircraft had set off – and it had left several hours ago. At this, our airfield manager immediately told the police and set in place the procedures for a missing aircraft. A few hours later we heard that the wreckage of a light aircraft had been found; even though the Search and Rescue services had experienced immense difficulty in reaching the sole occupant of the aircraft because of the appalling weather conditions, they had eventually managed to free him and rush him to hospital with severe, but survivable, injuries.

It was clear that the speed with which the pilot was rescued could only be attributed to one single factor – that on this occasion he happened to have a friend waiting for him at his destination. The aircraft could be located and the pilot rescued so quickly because we knew which airfield he had come from and could therefore trace the ATC units that he had spoken to en route, thus giving the emergency services a fairly good idea of his position when he crashed.

If the man had not been waiting for the pilot then we would have had no idea that an aircraft was inbound to our airfield, so the only information available to the rescue services would have been the location of the walkers in the mountains who thought they heard the crash. As the sound would have been reflected all around the mountains it really could have been coming from any direction, so the rescue mission would invariably have taken much longer. The airfield that the pilot had departed from would not have been expecting him back for several hours anyway, so would have had no reason to raise the alarm until much later in the day. The pilot would therefore have been trapped in the crash wreckage, on top of a mountain, in the middle of winter, for hours and hours – perhaps even all night – and had this been the case, given the temperature, he would have been lucky to survive at all.

This extremely serious event really does demonstrate the need to keep people informed of our whereabouts and our plans every time we go flying. Tell ops, write it in the tech log, but most importantly telephone the airfield you are planning to fly to and tell them. They may not require PPR, and when you speak to them they may say that you don't need to tell them your details or when you are planning to arrive, but tell them anyway. Even if the person you speak to doesn't write it down, at least you will then be in the back of their mind, so that if someone later asked them if any aircraft had been due in, they would say yes. You will probably not usually have someone specifically waiting for you at your destination, so even if you personally do not have chance to make the call, ask ops to make it for you. There may just be a day when you are very grateful that you did.

Interactions with Students

How you interact with your students will largely determine how successful you are at being a flying instructor: you could be the most talented pilot in existence, but if people don't want to fly with you, then you are probably a poor instructor. The students with whom you interact in your job will range from those who are your regulars, to someone who has perhaps called into the flying school to talk about learning to fly, as a potential student. As a flying instructor you are providing a service to paying customers, and the customers at flying schools are paying substantially more for their 'service' than the customers in most other circumstances! With this in mind, you should try to be as professional as possible in all your dealings with the school's students, current or future, because ultimately they can choose

Maintain a positive and friendly manner with students.

which instructor they wish to fly with and you should be doing your utmost to ensure that they choose you.

Positive interaction with students begins with the very basics of being friendly and approachable, so from your first flight of the day to the last, smile! It is surprising how many flying instructors are regularly grumpy and seemingly miserable when they are at work. In a job where you can just keep yourself to yourself and get on with it this may not be so much of an issue, but when you are providing a service to a customer who is paying a large sum of money, it is a very significant issue. Sadly, these instructors exist at many flying schools and most of us have come into contact with at least one of them at some point. They invariably earn themselves a reputation for being grumpy and therefore students try to avoid having to fly with them. When a student does have to go flying with one of them, upon their return they can usually be heard asking ops if they could please fly with a different instructor next time!

Obviously everyone has a bad day from time to time and it is inevitable that you will sometimes not be in the best of moods. On such occasions, always try to maintain a professional and pleasant manner when dealing with your students so that they enjoy flying with you every time and look forward to their next lesson with you.

Smiling and being friendly is fundamental in your job as a flying instructor, but so too is the manner in which you conduct your actual teaching. After all, your students want their instructor to be friendly and pleasant, but primarily they want to be taught how to fly. You should bear in mind that your students will each have very different levels of knowledge and ability when they start their flight training, and this should be accommodated accordingly in their lessons. The main attribute you need to demonstrate will often be patience. People do generally try their best in their flying lessons and it is important that you recognize this fact and respect it. They are only having lessons because they have a desire to learn – if they already knew how to do it, they wouldn't be having lessons. If a student is consistently doing something wrong, remember that they will not be doing so on purpose. You should therefore try to be as encouraging and as supportive as you can throughout each lesson that you deliver, being patient, calm and totally in control of both yourself and the situation at all times.

I have known of instructors who act aggressively towards their students if they do things wrong, shouting at them and telling them off like naughty schoolchildren. This hardly portrays the image of someone who is in control and professional about their job, but rather an image of utter panic and chaos. If a student has made a mistake then they clearly need correcting, and there may be occasions when that correction must happen in a split second, but there are far better ways of achieving it than by impatiently screaming at them. If a student is doing something consistently wrong they are likely to be annoyed and frustrated with themselves which, in turn, will make them tense and even less able to succeed.

In order to conquer their problem, it is up to you to provide encouragement and reassurance to keep your student calm and relaxed, to explain or demonstrate again what is required of them, and to help them to achieve it. That is the fundamental purpose of your job, after all. Use positive phrases and always talk about what they are doing in a positive way, such as highlighting the things that they are doing well in addition to those that they need to improve upon.

You should allow the student to fly the aircraft whenever possible during their lessons, but if you have handed control over to them, don't then interfere; as a capable and professional instructor you should be relaxed enough for your student to be flying, without your hands all over the controls. Of course, you will constantly be monitoring your student's actions when they are 'in control', and ready to take control from them at a moment's notice if necessary, but do leave them 'in control' as much as you can. It will give them confidence in their own abilities but also confidence in your abilities as their instructor.

A student of mine once had to fly with another instructor, and during our next flight together she commented on how noticeable it had been during her last lesson that she did not actually 'have control' of the aircraft throughout the flight, because the other instructor never really let go of it! She said that this had made her feel nervous because it gave the impression that he was not confident enough in his own abilities to allow her to take control fully, even though she was quite far on in her training and was perfectly capable of doing so.

There will be many times when your students will arrive for their lessons armed with questions, or perhaps will have things they want to discuss after their flight. The time available for this may be limited, but do your utmost to give them your attention and answer their questions. If there is not the opportunity to do so there and then, maybe suggest that you could speak to them about it over the telephone later on, or at another time. Quite often students will have worries or queries that they need to clear up in their own minds, and as a professional and dedicated instructor you should do your best to help your students to sort these out.

Potential Students

Prospective customers will frequently telephone or call into the flying school in person, whether they are looking into learning to fly themselves, or just wanting to buy a trial lesson for someone as a gift. The courses available and prices of lessons are usually very similar at schools in the same area, so it is often down to the ops staff and instructors to make the difference as to whether they give their business to you or to the flying school down the road – and from your point of view, any new customer is a potential new student, even if they are only having a trial lesson for Christmas to begin with. You should therefore try to make yourself available to meet these people if ops ask you to, because prospective customers will really appreciate having the

Show potential students around the facilities and the aircraft.

opportunity to speak to an actual instructor, and it is in your interests to do so as it will often prove to be beneficial to you in the long run.

The majority of people who have taken the trouble to telephone or to call in will already be fairly certain that they want to learn to fly, and the reason for their call or visit is to try and come to a definite decision. Someone who is considering learning to fly will be aware that they are going to be spending a large amount of money at their chosen school, so they will want to feel at home and as if their custom is important to the staff. If they are made to feel like a nuisance, by either just being handed a brochure to read, or by being left unattended to wander around, they will decide not to learn to fly at your school and will simply telephone or walk into the next school on their list to see if they receive a more positive response. If, on the other hand, they are made to feel welcome and valued as a potential customer, they are highly likely to make a decision to sign up for a course at your flying school without hesitation.

The best way to help them make up their minds about booking their flight with you rather than with your competitors is to get them a complimentary coffee, show them around the facilities and, most importantly, sit them in one of the aircraft. This experience in itself can sometimes be the factor that makes their decision to sign up for a trial lesson or flying course. If they are already very interested in learning to fly, the excitement of sitting in a real aircraft and being shown and talked through all the instruments and controls is usually too much temptation for them to resist. Even though it may have only been a few minutes, you having taken the time and trouble to talk to them and show them around, they are more likely to want you to be their instructor.

CHAPTER 2
ORGANIZATION, PLANNING AND PUNCTUALITY

Being well organized contributes hugely towards being a successful flying instructor. The fact that you can fly an aircraft to a high standard and have a good rapport with your students will go nowhere if you are disorganized, because being disorganized will inevitably lead to your being stressed, late and unable to give your students the time and individual attention that they deserve – and that, ultimately, they are paying a lot of money for. As a flying instructor you will face an almost infinite number of variables affecting your day-to-day job, some of which you have complete control over and others over which you have no control whatsoever. It is therefore extremely useful to identify what all the variables are, tackle the ones that you can control and minimize the effects of those that you can't, in order to make your working life as efficient and as productive as possible. This, in turn, should make your working life as enjoyable as possible, and therefore as rewarding as possible for your students.

Being organized involves a great deal of thought and planning. If you are going to succeed in being organized you will need to plan everything, from obvious things like planning navigation routes to more obscure things like deciding first thing in the morning when would be a good time to eat lunch. The more that can be achieved in advance, the better, and many factors can be thought about and planned days, or even weeks, ahead. Some factors cannot be addressed until the day itself, but having already done much of the work you will have more time to spend on these last-minute essential tasks. The underpinning objective in being well organized is to achieve an efficient and punctual day's work that will minimize your time on the ground and maximize your time in the air, because this is where both you and your flying school earn the money, and where your students progress. Maintaining a punctual flying programme, however, is one of the biggest challenges you will face as a flying instructor, particularly on a very busy day.

You will be under constant pressure to keep your lessons to time so that not just your own flying programme, but probably also those of your colleagues, run smoothly. Your own punctuality will affect that of your colleagues because you will often be booked in to fly several different aircraft on any given day: if you arrive back late from your flight, the instructor booked in the aircraft after you will automatically be late for their flight. Needless to say, this is a situation that you should try to avoid whenever possible; apart from the inconvenience to everyone (customers and other instructors) when lessons are delayed, the cumulative result over a whole day's flying can be long delays for lessons booked in late in the afternoon, with the extreme case of the last flight having to be cancelled altogether because it has gone dark!

CAUSES FOR DELAYS

On a general basis there are situations that almost inevitably lead to delays, such as not having a long-enough slot for the particular lesson that you need to give, so it is prudent to identify these as early as possible and rectify them before they happen. On a daily basis, there are certain things you can do to minimize delays throughout your day. Of course there are also things that lead to you being delayed which are entirely beyond your control, and when this occurs you just have to make the best of the situation that you are in. We shall first look at the latter factors because although there is not a great deal you can do about them, you should always have them in the back of your mind in order to minimize their effects wherever possible.

Holds
It is inevitable that sometimes you will be held, and this applies equally whether it is a small airfield or a major airport that you are operating into, or out of. At a large airport you may encounter delays on the ground when you are held for commercial traffic prior to departure, or you may be held in an 'orbit' (usually on base leg) before being cleared onto final for landing. At a small airfield you may also encounter a hold on the ground when you are waiting to depart, and this can be particularly bad on a summer day when the circuit is busy; if there are six aircraft in the circuit (not an unreasonable number for a popular airfield) you can be waiting at the hold with one, after another, after another (after another) on final. If the aircraft are all performing 'touch-and-go's it is not quite so bad, but if they are all making full-stop landings you can potentially be there some considerable time.

Equally, you may be delayed when arriving at an airfield if it is very busy, and there will no doubt be occasions when you are asked to join overhead and have to position yourself 'downwind number five' in the queue. Also, in these situations, always be ready to go around just in case the poor soul waiting at the hold has given up and lined up to take off in front of you when you're on final!

Waiting for Fuel
Another factor that applies to any airfield, no matter how large or small, is waiting for fuel. Some airfields will have a self-service policy whilst at other

airfields you will have to wait for a refuelling person to come and do it for you, but either way you will often find yourself in a queue of several aircraft waiting to refuel. Where fuel is concerned, however, it is always worth the wait; there will be times when you desperately just need to go, and there will be a very strong temptation to set off and 'hope for the best'. Needless to say this is never a wise option, and even if waiting for fuel does mean being late back you must just accept that. It is a very true statement that the only time you have too much fuel is when you're on fire, and you will regret every second of that flight home if you have even the smallest doubt as to whether you have enough fuel to make it back. The only positive actions you can take to minimize being delayed due to refuelling are as follows:

- Some airfields prefer pilots to state their need to refuel when inbound to the field, over the R/T. Therefore, if you are planning to land away and think you will need to refuel, ask them about this when you telephone to book in. At many places it really will speed up the process once you have landed.
- If the fuel bay or refueller is available straight away, refuel the aircraft now. The cups of tea and bacon butties will be enticing you directly into the café, but do not give in to your stomach – you will regret it later on when you return to refuel, only to discover that there are now four aircraft in front of you in the fuel queue.

If fuel is available immediately, refuel straight away.

- If there is already a queue when you arrive to refuel, make better use of the time by going to book in and allowing your student to have a rest now. If you return to refuel a few minutes later and there is still a queue then you are no worse off, but the chances are that it will have gone by then, thus saving you the ten minutes' wait.

Just to highlight a safety issue, always bear in mind the time that your aircraft requires for the fuel to settle once the refuelling has taken place, in order to carry out the pre-flight fuel drain. With this in mind it is best to try to refuel as soon as you can, so that the fuel has had time to settle before you want to set off again.

Aircraft Technical Problems

If it really is not your day, you will have a full day's flying booked in, the sun will be shining, the wind will be blowing straight down the runway at 10kt ... and when you start the engine for your first glorious flight of the day, your aircraft will become unserviceable. Your aircraft could 'go tech' in a variety of ways, taking a variety of lengths of time to be fixed. The best scenario would be an aircraft with a minor problem at an airfield where there are engineers on hand, at a moment's notice, to sort it out, but unfortunately this is not always the case. Probably the worst scenario would be an aircraft with a more serious problem at an airfield where there are no engineers, if for example the aircraft has to fly to another airfield for its maintenance.

If you do have a technical problem you are likely to be placed somewhere in between these two scenarios, as most airfields do have some sort of maintenance facilities and engineers based there, but many of them do not work weekends (when you are most likely to need them) and at any time it is unlikely there would be someone available immediately to come to your assistance. Whatever your particular circumstances are, however, a technical problem is likely to lead to a short delay, at best, and at worst can mean your flight (or even whole day) is cancelled completely.

Spacing of Bookings

The majority of flying schools, however large or small, are in existence for one ultimate reason and that is to make money. They are businesses, and they need to utilize their time and resources as efficiently as possible in order to maximize profits. Of course, one of their primary tools in achieving this goal is you, the instructor: you too must be used effectively to achieve your maximum potential in terms of the flying time available to you in any one day (due to airfield opening hours, daylight hours, etc.) and the flights you have booked in. Even the shortest flight, such as a twenty-minute trial lesson, will take up a certain amount of time on the ground, both pre- and post-flight. This time may only be a few minutes, but it does exist. For long flights such as cross-countries, a far longer time is required on the ground for planning, checking planning, telephoning airfields and so on. These processes are covered in detail later on, but the fact remains that time is required on the ground in addition to the actual flying time required for the trip.

This fact becomes an issue when observing the booking sheets and booking policies used by different flying schools. Obviously, different lessons will require differing lengths of slot, but the crucial factor is the length of time allowed between slots. For a one-hour flight, for example, some schools will allow a one-hour slot, and as the booking sheet then begins to fill up, other one-hour flights will also be booked in around it. In theory this is perfect, as all the lessons are booked in back-to-back, maximizing the utilization of both the aircraft and the instructor. In reality, however, it is a disaster waiting to happen: the first flight will be on time but the second will inevitably be ten or so minutes late, and by the time of the third (yes, only the third) flight of the day there could well be a thirty-minute delay. Bearing in mind that in the middle of summer there could be six or seven flights booked back-to-back in one day, the delay by the time of the last flight could be several hours – all because there is no time allowed between slots.

Imagine yourself going flying, on your own, for a routine flight 'around the block'. Assuming you have already checked the aircraft out and fuelled it up (which takes ten to fifteen minutes in itself), if you now fill in the tech log, gather together all your belongings and walk out, then take your jacket off, strap in, organize yourself with kneeboard and headset (and maybe even a pen) and set about starting it up, you have probably already spent five or six minutes on the task. If you include the after-start checks and calling air traffic for taxi, it is going to have taken you, on your own, seven or eight minutes to achieve 'brakes off'. This does not, of course, allow for certain inevitabilities such as forgetting your headset and having to go back in for some oil, or for the windscreen cleaner, each of which adds precious seconds to the time required.

If you now factor into that the additional minutes needed on an instructional flight, introducing yourself to your trial lesson customer and possibly their accompanying 'interested observer', each of whom has the potential for, for example, having to go back for the camera or deciding they need to go to the toilet again, the time required is ever increasing. Add to that the time spent strapping them into the aircraft and showing them the essential safety items, it is definitely in the region of ten to twelve minutes before you will be anywhere near brakes off. So having finally got going on your flight, you eventually land, taxi in and park up, then spend five minutes walking back in, signing the appropriate 'certificate' and bidding your satisfied customers farewell. You will now fill in your tech log, dash to the toilet and run back into the waiting area to seek out your next customer, thereby starting the process all over again.

It is startlingly obvious that this flying programme is never going to be on time, as it assumes that the 'brakes on' time for the last flight and the 'brakes off' time for the next flight are the same, but they are not and they never will be. At the very least you need a ten-minute gap between bookings to allow for all of the above, and even this assumes that there are absolutely no other delays (which invariably there will be). It also allows no time whatsoever for briefing and planning, which are both vital parts of the overall lesson.

It seems so glaringly obvious and yet there are flying schools in existence that do operate this system, and I know this because I once worked at one of them. They think that their instructors are being deliberately awkward by always being late back from their flights, and cannot understand why they are always moaning about it. These are also the schools whose customers all leave to fly elsewhere, because they are so utterly sick of their afternoon lessons consistently being two hours late and then being rushed with no briefings or de-briefings, which are both very important parts of the learning process. If your flying school has a booking sheet organized in this way there is very little that you, as their new instructor, can do about it, so good luck and brace yourself for the wrath of delayed students!

A sensible flying school will take into account the actual time needed between flights (as it really is a necessity, not a luxury), and allow for this when they book lessons in. They realize that a late customer is not a happy customer, and despite not being able to fit in as many bookings with this system, at least their customers will go away from their lessons happy and will therefore come back again. An example of this type of booking system would have ninety-minute slots for a one-hour flight, giving you the flexibility of fifteen minutes on either end, meaning that you will (hopefully) be able to do everything you need to do and still be back in time for your next slot. If your school does operate this system, however, don't become blasé: it may seem like you can relax with all the time in the world, but even with these slots, when you have a full day of flying booked in you will have done extremely well if you are on time by your last flight, as there is still no allowance made for any additional delays.

Students Arrive Late for their Lessons

This applies mainly to trial lesson customers who are unlikely ever to have been to the airfield before, rather than to students, but it can be a significant factor if you have a whole day of them booked in. The primary cause of this is that most flying schools are very difficult to find by road and this applies equally whether it is a flying school on a tiny grass strip, or one within the vast complex of airport buildings at a major international airport. Many people will travel a long distance to an airfield for their flying lessons, which involves the inherent risk on any long journey of being held up. Even those who live nearby can often drive round for an hour trying to find the place, usually involving one or more mobile phone calls from their car to your office saying 'I'm here – how do I get there?' Be aware of the frustrations of such an experience and greet them with sympathy, rather than impatience, when they finally do arrive!

The Weather

It is inevitable that the weather will cause delays from time to time. Although there is nothing that anyone can actually do about it, there are methods and strategies for managing the different situations it creates, and these are looked at later.

Your Aircraft is not Back

Just as your own delays and problems, discussed in this chapter, will mean that you are late back for the next person who is booked in your aircraft, so their identical delays and problems will mean that they are sometimes late back for you.

LONG-TERM AND SHORT-TERM PLANNING

Having looked at some of the factors affecting your day that are beyond your control, we shall now concentrate on the factors that you can control, as these are really the important ones. They fall into two clear categories: those that you can think about and plan for in advance, and those that you can only plan for on the day itself, so we shall refer to these categories as long-term planning and short-term planning respectively.

LONG-TERM PLANNING

In order to be able to plan and prepare thoroughly, it is necessary to spend a few minutes at the end of your working day – or perhaps during a spare half hour – looking through the booking sheets to see what has been booked in over the forthcoming days and weeks. Obviously, bookings are taken on a daily basis and therefore the contents of the booking sheets will be constantly evolving, but it is still worth a look to see what has already been booked in. What you are looking for at this stage is anything that might cause an obvious problem when the day arrives, because these problems can usually be avoided if they are noticed and rectified early enough in advance.

Is there a Fundamental Problem?

Let us assume that we are to look at the booking sheet for this time next week. The first factors to consider are those that will have a fundamental effect on any flight due to take place. They may dictate whether a particular aircraft can be used, whether a particular route can be flown or whether a particular airfield can be visited. This can be critical if the aircraft in question is the only one of its type available at your school, if the airfield in question is your home airfield, or if the airspace normally used by your school for flight training is affected. When studying the booking sheets, therefore, you must start by asking yourself the following questions:

Will the airfield I need to use be licensed?
This is extremely important, as all training flights for the issue of a PPL or NPPL must be conducted at licensed airfields. Most large airports are licensed twenty-four hours a day every day of the year, but at smaller airfields the

situation can be very different. Some airfields will only be licensed during specified hours on weekdays, some may only be licensed during certain times at the weekend and others may operate a combination of the two. Frequently, however, small airfields are not licensed at all on Bank Holidays or over Christmas and the New Year. This is a highly significant fact, because Bank Holidays are often some of the very busiest days a flying instructor can have; there has been many a Bank Holiday weekend when I have been planning where to take my student on the Monday, only to suddenly remember that out of my three choices of local airfields, two are unlicensed and one is closed altogether.

Equally, the Christmas and New Year period can be very busy, when people have time off work and want to cram in as much flying as possible. As long as you are well organized and have thought about it in advance, however, you can come up with an alternative destination, or an alternative lesson altogether, to fit in with the circumstances. The UK AIP (*see* Useful Information for details) and most VFR flight guides will provide information on normal airfield licensing hours. However, these may be subject to change, particularly over Bank Holidays and Christmas, so the best way to check in advance whether an airfield will be licensed on a particular day or at a particular time is to telephone them and ask. You could, of course, check the NOTAMs, but relevant information may not appear here until the day before, or even the day itself, and it would be beneficial to know much earlier than that in order to make your plans accordingly.

It is worth noting that an airfield being open and busy is in no way an indication of it being licensed: many airfields remain open and active long after they have become unlicensed for the day. This is something to bear in mind, especially during the summer months when the days are long and you may have lessons booked in until eight or nine o'clock in the evening. On such days five o'clock feels like the middle of the afternoon, yet many very busy airfields become unlicensed at five o'clock. It is very easy to forget about this when you are busy, and continue flying circuits or maybe send your student for some solo circuits. Other people are still flying and nobody would have any reason to question your actions as they would just assume that your student already has a licence and is merely flying with an instructor to revalidate it, or for some practice.

This is a potentially disastrous situation, however, because apart from the fact that it is an illegal flight, an unlicensed airfield generally means there is no fire cover – so what happens when your student misjudges the landing and collapses the undercarriage? There will not necessarily be a fire crew or any rescue services at all on the airfield to call upon for assistance. This is definitely a situation to be avoided, so always ensure you are flying from a licensed airfield.

Are there any events on that day to be aware of?
During the summer, there are fly-ins and air displays going on somewhere every weekend. Major events will have been notified in advance by Mauve

AIC and NOTAM (*see* Useful Information for details), and people are generally made aware of them through articles in the aviation press or posters to advertise the event. There are sometimes also much smaller events that attract far less – or even no – publicity and it is these that must be discovered and avoided, except as a consenting participant. A good example is a model-aircraft flying event, or an aerobatic competition: both these events will no doubt be common knowledge within their own fraternity of enthusiasts, but may not be widely known about outside of these groups. The organizers may have relied solely upon the efficiency of the hosting airfield to promulgate the information by issuing a NOTAM. Most airfields are very reliable in NOTAMing any unusual goings-on within (or above) their grounds, but it is also worth telephoning the airfield to make absolutely sure, as a NOTAM may not be issued until much nearer the time.

Flying displays (on all scales) can also occur out in the open, miles away from any airfield; it might be one fly-past of a single aeroplane or a twenty-minute display by the Red Arrows, but whichever it is you do not want to inadvertently find yourself in the middle of it. These displays should all be promulgated by NOTAM, but take particular note of the exact location. It will be stated as the name of the town or village where the display is taking place (which you may or may not be familiar with) and the co-ordinates of this place (which you may need in order to find it!). You should also pay attention to the start and finish time of the display (stated in Z on a NOTAM) because they will usually only last for a few minutes and you may find that it will not affect you anyway.

If you do come across some information about an event at an airfield or elsewhere, whether you found out about it from an AIC, a NOTAM, a poster or through word of mouth, do let others know: leave a note about it on the notice board and tell ops, so they can pass the information on to other flying instructors and members. Even if other people are aware of it, it can do no harm, and just because they were aware of it a week ago doesn't mean it won't have slipped their mind when the day comes.

Are any of the aircraft I am booked in nearly due for a check?
This is a factor that can cause major problems and disruption to the flying programme. Have a look at the tech logs and see if any of your aircraft are approaching their hours (or date) for a check, be it a 50-hour check, a 150-hour check or an annual. If the aircraft has 20+ hours remaining then there should not be a problem, but if, for example, it needs to have a check in 10 flying hours' time and the engineers need a couple of days' notice to start work on it, will it be out of hours by the time you are scheduled to fly it?

Booking the aircraft in for a check is the ever-impossible task of trying to see into the future: if the weather is good those hours will be used up in two days, so it will need its check in three days, but if the weather is bad it will not need its check until the weather is good again, which could be next week. The flying school will want to use up every last remaining hour before the check, as

Be aware of the number of hours left on the aircraft.

any hours left over will be wasted, so will not want to book the check too early in case the aircraft does not fly. Equally, the school cannot delay the check in the hope that the hours will be used up in case the aircraft flies them off straight away and then has to wait for its check, unusable, until next week.

The responsibility of sorting all this out lies with the ops department, but it may affect you if the aircraft you were booked to fly is suddenly unavailable. If so, bookings for that aircraft will have to be either cancelled or swapped around to fit in elsewhere. If all the school's aircraft are of the same type (or similar) it is not too difficult, as the lessons can usually be slotted in somewhere. If, on the other hand, the aircraft types are very different, this can be very difficult. Trial lessons can be taken in any aircraft, so they are easily dealt with; licensed pilots may be able to take the other aircraft type if they are already checked out on it (or this gives them the opportunity to be checked out on it, if they want to); but it is the poor students who are often left without an aircraft.

It is just about acceptable to take a student for a lesson in a different aircraft type if it is an early lesson where you are really teaching the basic principles, rather than the fine details and, primarily, if they are happy to do so. It would not be acceptable, though, if the student was quite far on in their training – flying circuits or doing solo work. It would be unfair to take them in a completely different type of aircraft as they would not learn anything new, but rather would re-learn what they had already learned from their usual type.

Your only course of action would be to give them the choice of either cancelling their lesson, or taking the other aircraft as an introduction to flying a new type, especially if it was one they wanted to fly anyway at some point (such as a four-seater rather than a two-seater). Many people would elect to go ahead with the flight for this reason, but if they chose not to go then that is their decision and they will be grateful that you gave them the option. To minimize the problems brought about by aircraft running out of hours, always pay attention when you are completing the tech log and if you notice that the hours are getting low, tell ops straight away. They will probably be aware of it already, but sometimes it can go unnoticed. By being vigilant you may just avoid the situation where someone casually mentions the fact that 'it's only got an hour left on it' at the start of a busy weekend.

Study your Bookings

Having established that there are no fundamental problems to affect your day a week from now, have a closer look at your bookings to see what each flight actually consists of. If you have a day of trial lessons then you will know exactly how long each flight should be (normally thirty minutes or one hour) with minimal time needed on the ground for each one, which is very straightforward. Alternatively, if you have a day of students then this will require a great deal more thought as their lessons will vary enormously depending upon the particular stage they are at in their training.

First of all, get out the student records for the people you are booked to fly with and see where they are up to in the syllabus. If it looks like some solo flying will be involved, whether circuits, general handling or navigation, check that the student has a current medical and passes in the relevant exams (depending upon your school's particular requirements for solo flying). Even if the person is one of your own students it is still prudent to check these things – there is always the possibility that they may have come in and flown with one of your colleagues, or passed a written exam on your day off or when you were out flying with someone else. You then need to check whether any of your students on this day has a lesson booked in between now and then (as many people do fly more than once a week) so that you can form a definite picture of the lesson you will be giving them by the time next week arrives.

Now that you know what your day is likely to consist of you can think about each flight in more detail, and this can be broken down into three parts for each lesson:

1) Time needed by you
 – for briefing
 – to check the aircraft out yourself
 – to check student's planning
 – to check weather/NOTAMs and to telephone airfields (for actuals and to book in)

2) Time needed by student
- – for walkround
- – for planning
- – for aircraft checks, R/T procedures, etc.

3) Time needed for the flight itself
- – time airborne
- – any time downroute (booking in/refuelling)

If any of your students is very early on in training, or perhaps about to start on navigation, it is highly probable that there will also be additional time required for demonstration and explanation of one or more of the following:

- walkround
- internal checks
- R/T procedures
- navigation planning

With all this in mind, you can now work out how long you are going to need for each specific flight and therefore whether the slot you have been allocated will actually be long enough for everything that needs to be done. On an average day, it is unlikely that you will have sufficient time for absolutely everything, especially if this includes activities such as an explanation of the R/T procedure at your airfield, or a thorough demonstration of navigation planning. If this is the case, and you believe that you are really not going to have enough time for one or more of your flights, then now is the time to act to give yourself the best chance of successfully completing your lessons on the day.

There are two approaches to achieving this: either to reduce the amount of time you will need on the day (by doing as much as possible beforehand, or on a different occasion) or to extend the slot you have been given for each particular flight. In practice, it may be necessary to use a combination of the two. Ask yourself: what can I do to minimize the amount of time I will need on the day? There is a huge amount that you can do beforehand to prepare for a lesson and to keep the time needed on the day to a minimum.

a) Plan exactly what you are going to do
Having studied the student records and found out what lessons you will be giving on the day, you can now make preparations for each specific flight in detail. Such preparations might include:

- Deciding on a navigation route to fly and which airfields to visit.
- Photocopying relevant airfield layouts.
- Photocopying R/T sheets that may be needed for the route.
- Obtaining a copy of any necessary forms (e.g. qualifying cross-country)

and placing them in the student's record so they can't be forgotten on the day.

- Thinking of a suitable alternative lesson if the weather is unfit for this one but is still suitable for others.

b) Tell the student what they will be doing

As the instructor, you are only half of the equation; in order to be properly prepared for the lesson, the student will also need to be fully informed of your plans so that they can organize themselves accordingly. Telephone them as soon as possible, to give them the maximum amount of preparation time, and ask them to:

- Read up thoroughly on the exercise to be flown.
- Draw the navigation route on their chart (including drift lines, half-way points, etc.).
- Write out their pilot's log in detail.
- Study the route to get an idea of what they should expect to see, and think about R/T calls, checks, joining procedures, etc.
- Read up briefly on the alternative lesson, if the weather is unfit for the planned lesson.
- Arrive at the flying school in sufficient time to complete the planning (e.g. put wind on) and the pre-flight checks, in order to get airborne punctually.

If the student is at an early stage of their training or ready to start on navigation, the extra tasks should ideally be carried out in advance of their lesson. In this case, ask them if they would have the opportunity to come in to the flying school prior to their booking, to go through:

- aircraft walkround checks
- aircraft internal checks
- R/T procedures and phraseology
- navigation planning

All these activities are absolutely necessary but each will take thirty minutes to an hour if explained properly; it is far preferable to do them thoroughly on another occasion rather than try to rush through them hurriedly before a flight.

If you still think that the slot you have been given for a particular lesson is too short to achieve what you need to achieve, even despite your best efforts to prepare everything for the lesson in advance, then you will need to try to extend your slot to give yourself more time. Anything that involves moving or altering bookings in any way should always be discussed with ops first: you will quickly become unpopular if you are seen to be changing what is booked in the booking sheet, because any changes made to your bookings will

A thorough demonstration of the pre-flight check is essential.

invariably affect other instructors' bookings. By far the best course of action is to talk to ops, explain what your problem is and what you would like to change, and let them do the changing.

Another important issue to consider before any changes are made is the availability of your student on the day in question. I once spent an hour trying to reorganize a fleet of aircraft and instructors to accommodate a longer slot for a qualifying cross country, and when I telephoned the student to tell him that I had successfully accomplished this feat, he said 'Oh ... I've got to go to the dentist at three o'clock – that's why I only booked in until two...'. Find out what their plans are for the day, before and after their existing slot, so that you know exactly what you have got to work with before you start re-arranging everything.

The scope of your alterations will depend entirely upon the other bookings for yourself and for the aircraft on the day. If there is a slot available immediately after your current slot, then it should be very simple to extend your current slot into the next one. If there is no time available after your current slot but there is some time available prior to your current slot, you could use some of that time so that your student's lesson will start earlier.

It might be that the only reason you have to be back at a certain time is because the aircraft you are booked in is needed back for another flight – is there another aircraft that you could use, which is available for longer? If there is no way of being able to have an aircraft for a longer time, are you available before the flight? If you are on the ground, the student could come in earlier in order to brief and to plan so that as soon as the aircraft becomes available you are ready to launch. If the student is quite far on in their training, they could arrange to come in early to do their walkround and planning on their own, even if you are still airborne on your previous flight, so that as soon as you return there are a minimal number of tasks left to do. Whatever the circumstances enable you to do, once you have come up with a new plan, ask ops to telephone the student and tell them what it is. Even if it means they have to change their schedule slightly, people are normally willing if they know it will be to their advantage.

First Slot Problem

On a day when the weather is anything other than flyable, there will often be a tricky situation surrounding the first slot of the day. The problem occurs because there is no time for the students who are booked in the first slot to telephone the flying school to check the weather, drive to the airfield and arrive in time for their briefing, prior to their allocated slot time. If the first slot is at nine o'clock and the flying school office is staffed from eight o'clock, then the students booked in the first slot are in with a chance of ringing to check the weather and still arriving in time, if they live fairly nearby. If the office is staffed from nine o'clock, however, the students booked in the first slot will have to either arrive late (but knowing that their lesson is definitely going ahead) or just come in anyway in the hope that the weather is suitable – often to find that it is not. Neither of these outcomes is very helpful, but you will find that there are certain students who do specifically want to fly early in the day for various reasons, so you will need to organize yourself – and them – to overcome the problem.

The best way to achieve this is to arrange to telephone the student on the morning of their lesson and tell them whether or not their flight will be going ahead. If you speak to them in advance of their lesson and explain the situation they will be very grateful of being saved a potentially wasted journey on the day. Decide on a mutually convenient time to make the call, and the specific phone number to use (e.g. their mobile if they don't want their entire household awoken at seven o'clock on a Sunday morning!), ensuring that this is early enough for you both to then travel to the airfield and do all that you need to do in time for the first slot. On the morning in question, you can obtain all the weather information either from the Internet or by calling the Met Office (*see* Useful Information for details), make your decision on the flight, then telephone your student at the agreed time to tell them the news in good time for them to arrive for their lesson.

SHORT-TERM PLANNING

So, the day that you planned so carefully a week ago is finally here. When you arrive at work today, you can be content in the knowledge that you have been as organized as possible and have done everything within your power to make the day a success: your students are all fully prepared for their lessons, having studied their flight training manuals, planned their navigation routes and revised their checks and R/T calls. They all know exactly what time to arrive on the flying school doorstep, eager and ready to check the aircraft out, put the wind on their navigation plans and maybe even clean the dead insects off the windscreen without being prompted. (Now that would definitely be extra brownie points – and a miracle!)

You have been impressively organized so far, but if you are really to succeed in achieving a fantastic day of flying with seamless transitions from lesson to lesson, you must now spend a few minutes formulating a plan for the day ahead, and keep monitoring and updating this plan as the day progresses. What follows would appear at a glance to be an endless list of tasks and you may wonder how on earth you could ever have time to perform them all in a morning and still be ready to go flying in time for your first lesson of the day. In reality, it is true that you would be unlikely to be able to complete all of them, but each task will only take a few moments and each one that you do manage to achieve will help you to save time throughout the day. This will mean that your students will benefit from thorough and unrushed lessons, and that you in turn will benefit from being able to work steadily and happily, without haste and the inevitable stress of being late.

Obviously, a good start to this way of working is to arrive at the flying school in plenty of time to do all that needs to be done, so that from the moment you walk through the door you feel calm and prepared for the day ahead, rather than rushed, stressed and behind before you've even started. It is always worth remembering, however, that no matter how much planning, preparation and organization goes into a busy day, you will always wish that you had more time because everything always takes longer than you expect it to. All you can do is to know that you have done the best you can.

Decide When to Refuel the Aircraft

This may not be straightforward if you are booked in to fly the whole fleet at one time or another throughout the day (as will often be the case), but look at the flights you have booked in and decide at what points you will require a refuel. This will also allow you to assess whether you will need to uplift fuel when you are downroute at another airfield, and therefore whether you will need to take a means of payment with you. By having a refuelling schedule in your mind, you can use your time between flights efficiently. For example, instead of landing, taxiing in, parking and then realizing that you need fuel for your next flight (and having to get back into the aircraft, start up and taxi down to the fuel bay) you can taxi straight to the fuel bay after landing, then

Have a refuelling plan.

taxi back to the apron so that you are ready and prepared for your next flight.

If your flying school uses a bowser instead of a fixed fuel installation it is even more important to be organized and know when you are going to need fuel. It will often take ten or twenty minutes for ops to fetch the bowser from its secure compound and drive it over to the aircraft to refuel you, so they would much prefer to know about this in advance.

If you discuss your refuelling needs with ops at the start of the day then they can organize when they are going to go for the bowser, and will probably try to co-ordinate refuelling the other aircraft at the same time. If ops are too busy to have a discussion in the morning, write refuel alongside your bookings on the board in the appropriate places, or leave a note for them on the desk so that at least they know what your needs are. By having a refuelling plan, it helps everyone to be organized and keep the programme running smoothly: if you are flying several different aircraft in the day it is very helpful to know where they are up to with fuel, particularly if you are busy and changing from one aircraft straight into another one. If all the pilots were to make a note on the board of when a refuel is due or has been done, then you would know at a glance whether your next aircraft will have sufficient fuel for your next trip, instead of walking out all ready to go and discovering you have empty tanks, which can be very frustrating on a busy day.

On this point, it is worth finding out what is generally accepted at your flying school in terms of who has the responsibility of refuelling the aircraft – the last pilot at the end of their flight, or the next pilot at the start of theirs. This does not really apply where a fuel bowser is in use as the bowser will come to the aircraft, but with a fixed fuel installation someone has to taxi the aircraft there and back, which can sometimes take quite a few minutes. If you are very lucky you may have the luxury of an ops person who is available to taxi the aircraft down to the fuel bay, refuel it for you and taxi it back again, but normally it is left to the pilots themselves. It tends to be the case that a pilot should refuel at the end of their flight and then taxi back to the stand ready for the next pilot, so if this is the situation at your flying school, make sure you know about it – you will become very unpopular very quickly if you leave an aircraft for the next person with empty fuel tanks when they are expecting it to be full.

This system does mean there is the possibility of putting too much fuel in the aircraft for the next pilot, if they are taking passengers and baggage, making them overweight for their flight. This also applies to you if another pilot is refuelling the aircraft that you are about to fly. If you have any flights booked in that are going to require a specific amount of fuel, ensure that you brief ops fully and make a note on the board for other pilots to see. It is both time-consuming and awkward to de-fuel an aircraft, and that is assuming your flying school has the equipment to do the job. There are all manner of legal rules and regulations surrounding the de-fuelling of an aircraft, the containers to be used and the subsequent storage of the fuel taken out, so it is always an absolute last resort, if indeed it is an option at all. With thorough planning and organization, however, this situation should hopefully be avoided.

Decide When to Refuel Yourself

This sounds ridiculous, but it is not. On a very busy day there will be very few opportunities for you to eat something and there is nothing worse than having to go flying on an empty stomach. Look at your programme for the day and see when there will be a spare ten minutes to sit down and refuel yourself. Even if things don't quite go to plan and your spare ten minutes disappears, you absolutely must make time to eat something during the day: you will be of no use to anyone, particularly yourself, if you suddenly have to deal with an emergency or an unexpected complication in the air, as mentioned earlier. Also, you cannot be too fussy about when lunchtime is. If you had a good breakfast before you came to work but your only chance to have lunch appears to be at eleven o'clock in the morning, then so be it: if you leave it until later, then 'later' might end up being six o'clock in the evening; then you will regret it, so always eat whenever you can because that may turn out to be your only opportunity.

Telephone Airfields

At the start of the day, you must decide whether you need to book any circuits or instrument procedures at airfields where PPR is necessary, and this applies to any flight due to take place that day, even if it is not until late afternoon. There are many airfields that will only accept, for example, three aircraft in the circuit at any one time, and this can cause an obvious problem if you do not book early; as an example, one such airfield has three flying schools of its own based there so it very quickly reaches the point where ATC will refuse to accept any more for a circuit detail or ILS because all the slots have been taken. It is not so much of a problem if there are other options available to you, but you may be in a position where you need to go to a specific airfield because it is the only one open at that time, the only one without a crosswind or with the appropriate instrument facilities – if you can't go there, you can't go anywhere. So you must ensure that you book yourself in as soon as possible.

If the flight is not taking place until much later on you will still have to give an ETA when you telephone to book in, but if as the day progresses it becomes clear that the ETA will be incorrect, make sure you call their ATC back to amend it. In this situation you may find that you lose your slot but, you having initially booked in early, ATC are more likely to try to squeeze you in somewhere – even if it is not exactly at the time you requested. For the remainder of your flights you are still likely to need to telephone other airfields, both first thing in the morning and at various points throughout the day, to check the weather or to book yourself in (even if PPR is not mandatory, as discussed earlier).

This is a necessary task and can sometimes take a few minutes, first of all to find the relevant telephone numbers, make the calls (when their lines are frequently engaged on a busy day) and pass on the details of your flight. If you are rushing about in the morning or later on, moving directly from one student to the next, the best plan is to ask ops to make the calls for you – if they can see you are occupied and they have a few moments to spare, they will usually offer. If they are booking you in, all that they should need from you is an ETA for arriving at the airfield and your intentions once you arrive, as they will be able to find out the remaining information – aircraft type, registration, captain's name – for themselves.

You may be about to go on a lesson but are trying to check the weather at another airfield in preparation for the following lesson and cannot get through or, alternatively, do not have time to do so. In either of these situations you could quite legitimately leave a note of what you need on the desk and hopefully, by the time you return, ops will have obtained the information for you (as it is, after all, in everyone's interest to keep the programme running smoothly). You must ensure that you always communicate fully with ops and keep them informed whenever you need them to do something for you, however; no matter how obvious something that needs doing may seem to you, they have got their own jobs to do. Never just assume that they will know what you need doing, because they won't.

Have a File

Throughout your working day there will be many moments when you need to show an airfield layout to a student, refresh their memory on a particular radio call or quickly photocopy a solo cross-country form before your student sets off on a flight. All the information you could possibly need will be located somewhere in the flying school, but when time is of the essence you do not want to have to spend twenty minutes searching for it, nor have to fight your way into the ops filing system to find a specific (and very important) item of paperwork. It is an infinitely better idea to have your own file, stored somewhere which is easily accessible to you (especially when you are in a hurry) and containing a master copy of every form, sheet and diagram that you are likely to need. It may take you a while to build up a file such as this, but an hour of photocopying on a quiet day will be time extremely well spent in the long run.

Items that would be useful in your file are:

- Airfield layouts for your base airfield and those airfields most frequently visited on navigation trips (usually two or three different places).
- Airfield telephone numbers, and other telephone numbers e.g. for sending flight plans, CAA, Met Office if website down, AIS for NOTAMs/Royal Flights if website down.
- Specific joining procedures for airfields used (this can be obtained from the AIP, but the information is often issued by the airfield itself).
- Sunrise/sunset tables, for quickly finding out when official night is.
- DOCs for local navigation aids.
- Radio Sheets
    - R/T outbound from base airfield
    - R/T en route, e.g. for FIS, RIS, MATZ penetration
    - R/T for approach and join at an airfield downroute
    - R/T in the circuit
    - R/T inbound to base airfield
- Forms
    - qualifying cross-country certificate
    - solo navigation form
    - solo circuit form
    - blank student record form (if someone has used the last one)
- AIC on content of dual flight with instructor (for reference).
- AIC on revalidation/renewal requirements (for reference).
- Checklists for yourself, such as when sending student on qualifying cross-country.
- Reminders to yourself, such as unusual places to visit, or navigation aids to use.

(*See* Useful Information for sample forms and details of where to obtain the above items.)

Obviously, much of this information will only be current for a relatively short time and should be updated regularly (e.g. AICs). It is, however, still worth having a copy of all these things to hand so that you can grab them, use them and go. The airfield layouts are vital for students, whether of your base airfield or of any other airfield they are visiting. Also, the airfields' telephone numbers are vital for you to call about the weather and to tell them that you are flying in. Other telephone numbers are very useful to have to hand such as the CAA (for when someone calls in with a complicated licensing query), the number to send Flight Plans to, and the Met Office and AIS for days when their website, or your computer, is not behaving. Radio sheets are invaluable for students (as discussed later) and copies should be kept of calls outbound from and inbound to your base airfield, calls in the vicinity of, approaching and joining another airfield, calls in the circuit, and en route calls such as when requesting a FLS, RIS or MATZ penetration.

Forms are very important and each flying school will usually have its own form to be used in each specific situation. Usually, these will consist of a form to be completed prior to a student's first solo flight, prior to their first solo navigation flight and prior to and during their qualifying cross-country. Another form which is very useful to keep your own copy of is a blank student record form, to guard against that fateful moment of realization that someone (worst of all, you) has used the master copy and there is now not a single blank one in the building. Fear not – there is one in your file. The AICs on the subject of licence revalidations and renewals are often referred to and it is convenient to have copies of these in your file to show people, as it may not always be possible to use the flying school computer there and then to

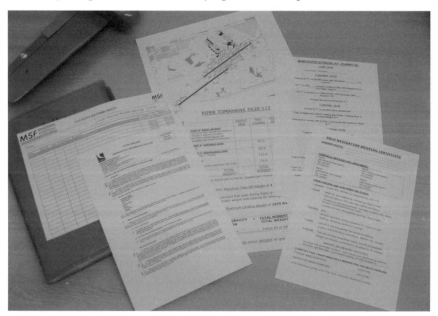

Keep a file of useful documents, forms and information.

print them off the AIS CD. Do check that you have copies of the very latest AICs, however, and ensure that you update them as necessary.

Your file can also contain notes and lists that you have made for your own reference, in addition to all the material you will need for your students. Such information might include a checklist for sending a student on their qualifying cross-country. For example:

Have I
- checked airfield opening times?
- checked sunset time?
- checked NOTAMs?
- telephoned all airfields to book the student in?
- given the student a qualifying cross-country certificate?
- given the student my phone number?
- checked the student has a copy of airfield layouts?
- checked the student knows where to go to book in/out?
- checked the student knows when/where to refuel?

This is not information directly for the student, but rather for your own reference. The items on this sample list are just some ideas: it is by no means exhaustive, but is nonetheless a good start when putting together a file. You will only really know what you need to have in your own file through the experience of needing something and wishing it was already in there; you will no doubt add to it from your own experiences of your students doing – or not doing – certain things that you want to make sure that subsequent students do – or don't do – in the future!

Other information for yourself might include details of free circuits available at an airfield on a certain day, or maybe a good place to visit that someone has told you about. It is very easy to become stuck in the habit of going to the same airfields, or using the same navigation aids, every day, and not even considering going anywhere new. If someone says they had a successful trip doing something different, make a note of it and you might just remember to try it yourself one day.

Write Briefs on the Board

This is not an issue if you use overhead projections or other media for your pre-flight briefs, but many flying instructors still like to write their briefs on a board. Some briefs can be very complicated and require a lot of time to write out, and this time may not always be available to you when you need it. If you have booked in sometime in the day a lesson whose brief will take quite a long time to draw out on the board (such as a first circuit session), then see if you have a spare few minutes to write the brief that may or may not be available just before that lesson.

For example, if your student's first circuit session is booked in at two o'clock, but you are unlikely to be back from your previous flight before this time, see if you have any spare time free earlier in the day. If you discover that you have a thirty-minute gap between bookings in the morning, why not write out your brief during this time so it is all ready for later on? In this situation it would be important not to completely hog the entire board space, but to leave room for other people's briefings in the interim period, and you must also make sure you write a note somewhere clearly visible to tell other people not to rub your brief off, for example 'brief in preparation for 2pm flight' and the date, not just 'today'. If you do not do this then someone else may well assume it is a brief that has already been used, and erase it.

Monitor the Time

As your working day progresses you will be able to clearly see how your programme is working out. Ideally, it will be exactly as it should be – perfectly punctual with time for relaxed briefings and maybe even a cup of tea – but sadly, despite your very best efforts, this is not always the case. If your bookings are organized sensibly then a few minutes of delays here and there should be able to be absorbed into the gaps between bookings, so that the lessons at least manage to remain within their own slots. If there is a major delay, however, such as an emergency at the airfield or an aircraft technical problem when all the aircraft are booked up all day, you may find that your lessons are now overlapping and it is unavoidable that all your subsequent flights are going to be, for example, an hour late. In this case, look at your bookings: if it is a fairly quiet day, there may well be some large gaps between lessons (e.g. an hour) that will absorb the problem, but if it a busy day this would be very unlikely.

With no way of making up the lost time, you will need to come up with a plan of what to do before any more of your students set off from home for their lessons which are now late. It is far better to delay someone whilst they are still at home than to let them arrive and then tell them there is a long delay. Chances are the next student will already be at the flying school waiting for you, so there is nothing you can do about them, but you need to intercept your later students as quickly as possible. Ask ops to telephone the remaining students and explain the situation, apologize (although it is nobody's fault, just one of those things) and ask if they would be able to come in later. Some may say no they can't, in which case they will unfortunately have to be cancelled altogether, and others may say that they'll come in at the original time anyway and wait at the school, which is fine.

Unavoidable delays do occur in aviation and there is absolutely nothing anyone can do about them, but so long as you have given your students as much warning as possible that their lesson will be late, then there is nothing more that you can do about it. It is infinitely preferable to saying nothing and allowing everyone to arrive for their lessons as normal, only to then discover that they are an hour late, so that when you return from your flight the school is full of irritated and annoyed students whom you then have to try to teach.

TO SUMMARIZE

If you have thought about your day in advance, planning it in detail together with your students, then been as organized as possible on the day itself, you have the best possible chance of having an enjoyable, productive and stress-free working life. There will always be external factors that influence your work and over which you have absolutely no control, but if the controllable factors have been dealt with then at least the effects that the uncontrollable factors have on your day should be minimal.

A final point to take into account is that no matter how infinitely hard you try to be organized and punctual, you will inevitably discover that everything in aviation always takes longer that you think it will. With this in mind, don't be too hard on yourself if you find that, despite your very best efforts, you are late. Some days there is just nothing you can do about it, and as far as your students are concerned, if they are intending to become involved in the weird and wonderful world of aviation, it will do them good to learn this fact sooner rather than later.

CHAPTER 3
STUDENTS

Your students will consist of different types of people from different backgrounds who are having flying lessons for different reasons and, in general, most students will get on with most instructors, and vice versa. They will range from someone who has no intention of obtaining a licence, but who just wants to grasp the basics, for the experience, to someone who wants eventually to become a pilot as a career. You will have to adapt your teaching technique to cater for each student's individual personality, preferred learning methods and actual ability (both on the ground and in the air) in addition to guiding them through the hard work, frustration and elation involved in conquering a new skill. Your students are all paying a lot of money in return for your time, knowledge and patience: you must endeavour to make their time with you as productive and as comfortable, but above all as enjoyable, as possible. If you succeed in accomplishing this, you will often find that your students become permanent friends.

TIMESCALES OF LEARNING

Most students will be having flying lessons with the aim of obtaining a pilot's licence, whether a JAR PPL or a NPPL. Usually they are fitting this around their current job, so they will book their lessons for the weekend, or for a day off in the week, and are happy to progress at this steady pace without any particular timescale in mind. Other students may prefer to follow a tightly scheduled course, flying several times a day in order to try to obtain their licence in as short a time as possible. Either way, your input in terms of ground briefings and airborne lessons will be the same and the student's success or failure in achieving their goal will be determined predominantly by their own input.

Commitment
You will come across vast differences in the amount of commitment to learning to fly that your students appear to have. Some students will arrive for their lessons thoroughly prepared and having read all the books (and made notes), whilst others won't have given flying a thought since their last lesson. There are many reasons for this difference in approach, usually linked to your students' lives outside of aviation. If you have a student who is retired and has always wanted to learn to fly, the chances are they will have had the time to read up the relevant sections of their book ready for their next lesson. For

another student, their actual lessons may be the only time they have available to dedicate to flying, away from their demanding job, family or other commitments, so they will not always arrive for their lesson having done any preparation. This does not mean that they aren't taking it seriously or aren't dedicated enough, as quite often they would love the opportunity to spend more time on their flying, but it may just be the circumstances they are having to work around.

You may have another student who seems to lack commitment altogether. A frequent example of this is where a parent insists that a daughter or son should learn to fly, but in fact the daughter or son has absolutely no interest whatsoever in doing so. They are reluctantly brought for their lessons, but that is the extent of their involvement in the learning process and you know that they will not have read up in preparation for their next lesson, even if you had asked them to.

Whatever your student's circumstances, you must make it clear to them that their progress through the flying course will inevitably be hindered if they do not read their books. This applies to each flying exercise that is taught throughout the course, because in reality there are rarely opportunities to give long briefings: if the student has read about the theory of the lesson beforehand, then their pre-flight brief will make far more sense.

This also applies to the ground examination syllabus, as someone could physically learn to fly an aeroplane perfectly well having never opened a book on the subject, but unless they have also passed all the written exams they will never earn their licence. Whether your students are eager to study and learn or reluctant to do so, it is your responsibility to tell them how vital the studying is – and keep telling them, at every lesson! Indeed, you will sound like a school teacher nagging your pupils to do their homework, but that is exactly the role that you are in and if you have made it unequivocally clear to them from the start then there can be no comebacks: no-one can blame you if a student is ready for their first solo but can't be sent because they have not yet passed their Air Law exam. On occasions you really will despair about this, but once you have clearly explained to your students the need to study, whether they choose to do so or not is their own decision. Ultimately, you can't pass their exams for them – the hard work has to come from them.

Continuity

Continuity is one of the most important factors in determining the rate at which someone who is learning to fly actually progresses. Whether the person is a naturally gifted pilot or not, they will progress much faster if their flying lessons are closer together, rather than further apart. This should be explained to all your students from the outset as they may not realize how significant the continuity of their lessons really is. Once it has been explained, this factor alone may even determine whether they start training now, flying once every few weeks, or wait until they have saved the money to have lessons more regularly. In an ideal world it is preferable for your students to fly every single day so that they don't have the chance to forget anything from their last lesson, and therefore make the fastest possible progress. In reality this is rarely possible, and most commonly people book themselves in to fly once a week or so.

It should be remembered that the amount of continuity a student has is usually not a reflection of their dedication to learning to fly but more often a result of circumstances, such as the availability of time or finances for their lessons. Quite often a student who can only afford to fly once a month will spend the weeks between lessons reading their books and absorbing as much as they can whilst desperately waiting for the day of their next lesson to arrive, so in fact can be better prepared than someone who can afford to fly twice a week. As long as you have made them aware of the importance of continuity, then how they decide to organize their lessons is up to them.

Learning Styles and Progress

Each person will respond differently to different methods of teaching and learning, whether they are trying to learn something theoretical or a new practical skill. Flying is both of these things, so as a flying instructor you must try to identify how each of your students responds to the various teaching methods available to you, in order for them to make the best possible progress. The basic methods for ground teaching include verbal explanations, writing out or projecting explanations on a board, and the use of diagrams, computer-based explanations and models. Once airborne, you are limited to verbal explanations and actual demonstrations, with the odd scribble on your kneeboard if absolutely necessary. Most people have the ability to learn the knowledge and skills required to pilot a light aircraft successfully, but the speed with which each person does so can vary enormously. Some people pick it up very quickly, others slowly, and the majority are somewhere in between.

If, during one of your lessons, your student just doesn't seem to be 'getting it', try explaining it to them in a different way, or demonstrating the exercise again, perhaps one step at a time. If they are still struggling, return to the last exercise that they did successfully complete and spend a few minutes revising this before trying to progress again on to the new exercise. It may just be that they are having a mental block and a short break from it will help. If they really cannot grasp what you are asking them to do, then leave it for another time. The student will only become increasingly frustrated if they consistently fail to achieve something, so it is better to go over it all again on the ground until they do seem to understand, and then return to it on another flight. If this does happen, don't worry. It is very rare that someone does not eventually master learning to fly and nobody gets through the course without struggling with something. It just takes a good instructor to get them through their difficulties.

The secret is not to expect too much too soon. When you first start work as a flying instructor you have no frame of reference for the rate at which

Use an aircraft model to aid explanations.

students will normally progress, but you will quickly come to realize what the average ability level is and therefore recognize when a student seems to be 'a natural', or to be particularly struggling with something.

If you really feel as though you have tried everything but the student has still have not grasped it, ask another instructor to fly with them to see what response they get. Everyone encounters these difficult situations occasionally and sometimes the student will progress through their difficulties just by experiencing a fresh instructional technique. This is in no way a bad reflection on you, as every instructor will have slightly different methods of explaining things, and whilst most of these explanations will suit most students, there are certain times when a different person explaining something can suddenly make perfect sense. Alternatively, take the opportunity to talk to other instructors to see if they have any advice – they may have had a student with the same problem, which hopefully had an easy solution.

A perfect example of the usefulness of sharing experience in this way is a student I used to fly with. He suddenly developed great difficulty in judging the flare, despite having already been solo on several previous occasions. He experienced this problem whilst flying with me, and the same problem a few days later with his other instructor, and it was very puzzling as the problem had not occurred before.

One day, the student's other instructor and I were discussing the situation, and its possible causes, in the office. During this conversation one of our colleagues returned from a flight, and after a few minutes said 'Does this chap wear glasses?' The student did indeed wear glasses, and the question was then raised as to whether he had recently started wearing a different pair to those he had previously worn for flying. Out of curiosity we telephoned the student to ask him this straight away, and sure enough he said that yes, he had been wearing a different pair during his last two flights. Having never worn glasses ourselves, myself and the student's other instructor had not even thought about this, but our colleague (who did wear glasses) was well aware of the effect that wearing a different pair of glasses could have on a pilot's ability to judge the flare, as she had experienced it herself in the past. We told the student that this could have been the cause of his problem, and when he wore his old glasses for his next flight, his landings immediately returned to their normal high standard.

No matter what difficulties you may encounter when teaching someone to fly, you should always have the same underlying objective and that is for your students to enjoy themselves. If you were meant to be covering straight and level part two and you ended up spending the whole lesson revising straight and level part one because they had forgotten everything, so be it. You can only work at the pace that each individual student is capable of; there is certainly no point in rushing on with the next thing before they are ready, because they will feel overwhelmed and confused, and maybe start to doubt whether they are capable of learning to fly at all.

Your job is indeed to encourage your students to progress as much as they can on every lesson, but primarily it is to ensure that they enjoy their flying. You should always leave them 'on a high', even when they have made mistakes, and this applies both in the air and during their post-flight debriefing. Irrespective of how much of your planned lesson you managed to complete, if your students always leave you feeling that they have learnt something and enjoyed doing so, then you are doing your job correctly.

WELFARE

For every person that you fly with, the experience of being airborne in a light aircraft has the potential to be exhilarating but also, occasionally, unpleasant. Whether the person has never been airborne before in their life or whether they have thousands of hours logged in command, you may encounter times when they react unpredictably to the sensations. The majority will be perfectly happy and love every moment, but a few will find that it makes them feel uncomfortable and queasy, with a few of these being physically sick. There are, however, some methods for minimizing the chance of this occurring.

- Instil into your students (and encourage ops to mention to trial lesson customers) the importance of eating. People often think it better not to eat before flying but in reality the exact opposite is true. If they have had breakfast or lunch before arriving for their lesson, they will be able to concentrate far better and are far less likely to feel any effects of airsickness.

- Be aware of the weather conditions most conducive to airsickness occurring. These are days when it is turbulent and days when it is hazy. On a turbulent day common sense dictates that airsickness would be fairly likely, and it is usually associated with operating at low altitudes, on days with high windspeeds or high surface temperatures. As we know only too well, however, turbulence can occur on any type of day and at any level, and sometimes completely unexpectedly. Haze may not be such an obvious cause for airsickness occurring, but with no horizon to focus on, the brain cannot orientate itself with a horizontal reference; this leads to the same condition as sea-sickness, or that experienced when reading with your head down in a car. The worst case is a combination of the two, such as a very hot, thermally day with thick haze – and what do we have all summer when everyone wants to book their flying lessons?

  If it is hazy, try to find a level where you can see a defined horizon (usually higher up); if it is turbulent, try to find a level where it is calmer (also usually higher up). The effect of turbulence on the aircraft will be reduced by flying at a slower speed, so do this if the turbulence is really strong. Even if you are forced into haze or strong turbulence at the beginning and end of the lesson, most people can endure it perfectly well for a few minutes. It is just best to try to avoid it throughout the majority of the flight.

- Remember that every movement of the aircraft will feel exaggerated to someone who has never experienced it before, or is still early on in their training, so fly as gently as you can, maintaining mainly straight and level and limiting your turns to a shallow angle of bank to begin with. Always roll wings level for at least a few seconds in between turns, never rolling from a turn in one direction directly into a turn in the other direction, and always say you are going to turn (and in which direction) before you do so. Treat your students gently until they have adjusted to the environment, or until it becomes obvious that they are happy with the sensations and want to do more.

- Keep the aircraft cool. Just as someone is more likely to feel uncomfortable and queasy in a hot car, the same applies to an aircraft. For this reason I open all the air vents as soon as possible after start-up, because they are sometimes very difficult to operate once you are airborne, especially those in the back, and if it becomes too cold I can always close them again.

- Sitting in the back of an aircraft is much more conducive to motion sickness than sitting in the front. If you have someone in the back, and especially if they do not have a headset or intercom, always try to keep them informed of what is going on. Any feelings of nausea will be made worse by sudden unexpected movements of the aircraft, such as a turn or a climb, so tell them when you are going to manoeuvre the aircraft in order to prepare them for it. By doing this they will be concentrating on something, which should prevent them from feeling queasy, plus they will feel as though they are playing a more active part in the flight.

Be on Your Guard

Despite your best efforts to keep everyone in the aircraft feeling well, there will be times when they won't. Human nature dictates that very few people will actually own up to the fact that they feel ill, being far more likely to sit there as if nothing is wrong, perhaps until it is too late! Luckily, though, there are certain tell-tale signs that people in this situation tend to display, so hopefully you will be able to do something about it earlier rather than later, and possibly even prevent it altogether.

Firstly, they will go very quiet. This is sometimes difficult to detect as many trial lesson customers, and some students, are very quiet anyway. Ask them a direct question to see if you can elicit a response – a very brief answer may hint at a problem. Secondly, they will look pale. Again this is quite difficult to determine around the headsets and while trying not to stare at them too blatantly. If the paleness has reached the point where it is accompanied by beads of perspiration on their temples then you really do have a problem.

It is a strange effect of the human body that if someone plants the seed in your mind that you are going to feel sick, then you generally do, but if it is looking as though your companion is feeling the worse for wear, there are a few things you can do in an effort to improve the situation.

- Do not mention the word sick! This is only going to make things worse, so avoid it at all costs.
- Fly straight and level, limiting necessary turns to a very shallow angle of bank, and slow down to minimize the effects of any turbulence.
- Try to encourage them to take control. If they are made to concentrate on flying the aircraft, this should distract them from feeling nauseous.
- Tell them to look out and focus on the horizon (if there is one). This should help to reduce any sensations of sickness brought about by disorientation, or at least keep them to a minimum.
- Talk about mundane, everyday things that are totally unrelated to flying, in an attempt once again to take their mind off feeling unwell.
- Head for home straight away. As a large part of them feeling queasy is likely to be psychological, knowing they are trapped in a tiny aeroplane up in the sky with no escape, then if they can see that they only have a

few more minutes before landing they should feel better. You can back this up with reassuring comments about nearly being home and not having much longer to go now, pointing out how close the airfield is as soon as possible.

- Discreetly have some sick bags at the ready! Again, to blatantly thrust a sick bag in their hand will only cause them to feel worse and may actually provoke them into being sick when they might otherwise not have been. You do need to be on standby for the event, however, because the very last thing you want is to be rummaging around for a bag in the side pocket (amongst all the checklists, fuel drains and broken pens) if you should suddenly need one, but keep them out of obvious sight until the time comes. As mentioned later on, I like to ensure that there are several sick bags in each available pocket of the aircraft, plus some in my kneeboard, so there should always be one easily accessible at a moment's notice. It is also imperative that you personally can reach them, as in my experience people never get one out for themselves. Not wishing to dwell on the thought, it is also true that one is sometimes not enough, so always be prepared!

If the worst situation does occur and they are physically sick, all that you can do is make them as comfortable as possible, which means getting them on the ground as soon as you can. People usually feel extremely embarrassed and apologetic about it, so reassure them not to worry. Tell them that it happens to a lot of people and is just 'one of those things'. Meanwhile, you can make sure all the air vents are fully open and try to focus your concentration ready for landing!

STUDENT RECORDS

It is most likely that you will fly with students who are at various stages throughout their training, rather than starting off with students who are all right at the beginning. They may have been booked in with you because their usual instructor was already busy, they may want to try flying with a different instructor, or they may have come from another flying school altogether. Whatever the reason, you will now be relying on the information contained in their student record to give you the basic facts about where they are up to in the syllabus, in addition to a viewpoint on their strengths and weaknesses as a pilot so far, so that as their instructor you can judge which areas you need to concentrate on.

The records themselves are usually all stored alphabetically in a drawer and will contain a sheet for you to enter the details of each flight (date, aircraft flown, exercise covered, duration of lesson, total hours flown to date and instructor's comments) plus photocopies of the student's medical certificate, exam passes and any other relevant information. The majority of the details needed from you, therefore, are extremely brief and it is only your comments on the student's progress that will require some thought.

Student records are an essential part of an instructor's job.

What you write is entirely up to you, but you should try to make the comments useful to another instructor who may subsequently be reading them. I have frequently come across records which just say 'good', and when I am taking this student for their next lesson that does not give me a great deal to work from. I think the best one I ever read was 'Quite a nice day but no horizon', which was nothing more than a complete waste of ink. No student is 'good' at everything – everyone has strengths and weaknesses. You don't need to go into a minute-by-minute account of their entire lesson, but give a brief summary of the lesson that took place, including details of any navigation routes flown, what they did well and, more importantly, what they need to work on next time.

It is also useful to mention the exercise to be flown on their next lesson, because sometimes they may need to go over the same things again, or you may not have had a chance to complete everything and will therefore have to finish off the last exercise before moving on to the next. Remember that most of the time the next instructor who will be flying with one of your students will be you, and you will be making life so much easier for yourself when you come to plan their next lesson if you have a clear idea of what they did last time – especially if last time was several weeks ago.

Completing student records is an essential part of your job as a flying instructor, but at the end of a hectic day when you are tired, hungry and want to go home, the very last thing you will feel like doing is sitting down to write about every student you have flown with – it is sometimes difficult enough just to remember who you have flown with, never mind what they did! It is important that you do complete them, however, and ideally as soon as possible after the flight so that the details are still fresh in your mind, as these are so much more difficult to remember at a later date.

As the next instructor will make their own assessment of the student's progress, the most important thing is that you at least fill in the details of the exercise that has been done. There is nothing more frustrating than checking a student's record to see what you are going to teach them and spending time preparing for that lesson, only to discover when they arrive that they did that lesson last week – but their instructor failed to make any note of it in their student record. To ensure that you are about to launch into the correct briefing it is always wise to check the student's logbook when they first arrive, as people are likely to have filled the logbook in even if they did not fill the record in; but to avoid the inconvenience of this type of situation, always complete your student records.

CHAPTER 4
TRIAL LESSONS

Each trial lesson is a potential student.

At any flying school trial lessons will form a significant proportion of the bookings, and as a new flying instructor you are likely to spend a lot of your time taking them because other instructors will be busy flying with their own students. These flights are generally bought as gifts for birthdays, Christmas, retirement, and so on, so the school will usually provide some sort of gift voucher or certificate that the recipient will bring with them on the day of their flight. People who come along for trial lessons are a combination of male and female, old and young, experienced fliers and complete novices, so each one is unique and should be treated as such. Some trial lesson customers will be shocked when they arrive at the airfield, having been bought the flight as a one-off surprise gift and having no particular interest in aviation, whilst others will have bought the flight for themselves because they are seriously considering learning to fly. Ultimately, trial lessons are a large part of a flying instructor's job, which some instructors loathe and others love.

Thinking about my own vast array of trial lesson experiences, they range from a nine-year-old boy who spent all his time playing on his flight simulator because he was desperate to become a military pilot when he grew up, and did not want to have to come down, to a lady who was bought the flight as a surprise gift from her family to celebrate her eightieth birthday. She had never set foot in an aeroplane of any sort before in her whole life, and although she enjoyed it and was fascinated when we flew over her house, she had no desire to repeat the experience. She said that she was very pleased to have done it but 'once was quite enough'!

You will undoubtedly find that you are repeating yourself on trial lessons, especially if you have flown several on the same day, but you must always make a conscious effort to be as enthusiastic on the last as you were on the first; for many people it truly is a lifetime's ambition which they are not likely to repeat, so do your best to make it special for them. If you do a good job there is every chance that you will gain some more business for yourself, as many trial lessons are bought purely through recommendations to friends, family or colleagues. Also, no matter how interested in flying someone is when they arrive, you just never know who will be bitten by the bug: every single one is a potential new student, so make sure that they want you to be their instructor.

Some trial lessons are bought by people for themselves if they are interested in learning to fly, but most are bought as a gift for someone else. This means that the lesson is not normally booked in at the time it is purchased, enabling the person who has been bought the flight to telephone and book themselves in at a convenient time and date, once they have received their voucher. On other occasions, the person buying the lesson as a gift may book a time and date for the flight to take place, especially if the whole thing is intended as a surprise on the day for the person having the flight.

CONSIDERATIONS WHEN THE LESSON IS BOOKED

Whatever the circumstances and whoever the flight is for, however, trial lessons mainly consist of people who are totally unfamiliar with aviation and aircraft. A special effort must therefore be made to ensure that they are made aware of certain factors that they might not otherwise appreciate, and which could have a significant effect on their ability to undertake a flight in a light aircraft. In order to achieve this, there are certain questions that need to be asked at the time the trial lesson is purchased so that when the day of the flight comes you, as the pilot, are not suddenly presented with any unforeseen problems that could prevent it from going ahead. Generally, the ops staff will be armed with a list of information to pass on and questions to ask people who are purchasing trial lessons, but as you are the person who will be directly affected when the customer arrives for their flight, it is important that you are aware of these points too.

Travel Time

Before a slot is allocated for a trial lesson, it should be established where, geographically, the people will be travelling from on the day. If they live fairly close to the airfield then the slots they are offered can be flexible, but if they will have a long journey they should be encouraged to book a slot later in the day to avoid the inevitable 'first slot problem' discussed in Chapter 2; if your full day of flying is ever going to run on time, it is essential that your first customers arrive promptly!

Names

Having found a suitable slot, the name of the person who is having the flight should be taken – which will not necessarily be that of the person who is booking it – and their name written clearly in the booking sheets. Frequently, trial lessons are booked in someone else's name, which can cause a great deal of confusion when the day comes.

A contact telephone number should also be taken, with confirmation that this can be used on the day that the flight is booked in. This is very important as so often people will give an office number that is no use to anyone when you need to contact them urgently about their flight on a Sunday morning. On this point it should be clarified whether or not the trial lesson is a surprise, because if so a note should be made of exactly who to ask for in the unlikely event that the flying school needs to call. If the flight is a surprise and only a particular person should be contacted about it, a clear note of this should be made on the booking sheet.

Vouchers

The person should be advised to bring their voucher with them on the day, and the voucher number (or however they are referenced) taken, to clarify when the voucher was issued. Most schools will have the validity period clearly stated on their vouchers, but despite this there are many occasions when people try to use them when they are out of date, in some cases by several years! Each school will have its own policy for dealing with these situations, such as asking the customer to pay the difference in price from when the flight was purchased (as prices inevitably increase over the years) or perhaps by offering the customer a slightly shorter flight to take this price shortfall into account. When faced with this sort of option, most people will quite happily agree to it, realizing that they only have themselves to blame for not using their voucher within its (clearly stated) validity period.

There are some flying schools, however, that will not honour a trial lesson voucher if it is beyond its validity period and, equally, there are some customers who will not accept a shortened flight or will not agree to pay any difference in price from when their voucher was purchased. Either of these cases will often cause problems, so far better for the situation to present itself whilst they are on the telephone, so it can be sorted out straight away. The alternative is that the customer turns up on the day of their trial lesson, hands over their voucher and is then told that they can't go (or that they can only go if they pay extra – which they are not prepared to do), so having been standing there ready and waiting to take them for their trial flight, you now find that they are not going after all. You therefore lose your hour's flight, when you could easily have been booked in with someone else if all this had been sorted out in the first place when they telephoned to book.

Telephoning

They should be made aware of the importance of telephoning the flying school on the day of their flight to check whether or not it will be going ahead, to save any wasted journeys, irrespective of what they think the weather looks like: they need to appreciate the fact that there are certain weather conditions that may not be obviously apparent (such as the wind 'in the wrong direction') and that it is much better to telephone regardless of how nice the weather appears to be, just to make sure. It is quite amazing that people still insist on turning up for trial lessons (having not telephoned to check if their flight will be on, despite having been asked to do so) and when they are told it is not going ahead due to the weather they are shocked and make the classic comment 'but it looked like such a nice day'. Indeed it may do, but that does not necessarily make it suitable for flying.

The worst culprits for this type of occurrence are those days when your trial lesson customer will look up to see a beautiful clear blue sky so they will not bother to telephone, because to them it is obviously such a good day to fly. Upon arrival at the airfield, however, they will discover that they are going nowhere because the visibility is 3,000m in thick haze and all the aircraft are grounded – so as long as they had been told to telephone before setting off, you are completely absolved of responsibility for any wasted journeys that they may have (... and maybe they will believe you next time!).

Spectators

The number of 'spectators' they are allowed to bring should be clearly stated. At some flying schools this will not be an issue if there are spacious premises, a café or places to sit and wait, but at certain schools where there is limited space, or perhaps where people need 'escorting' by a member of staff when outside, trial lesson 'spectators' can be a real problem. As long as they are clearly told what the situation is in advance, however, any problems on the day should be avoided.

Food

The importance of not flying on an empty stomach should be mentioned to make sure that the customer has eaten something before they arrive. Again, people who don't know assume it is best not to eat, but this will accentuate any discomfort caused by turbulence and thus nausea will be much more apparent. Often the only food available at the flying school will be chocolate bars, so it is important that they have had something substantial (i.e. breakfast or lunch) before they set off.

Much of this information is likely to have been mentioned in the paperwork accompanying the voucher, but it is always better for these important points to be reiterated.

In terms of general physical issues, people booking trial lessons should also be informed about not flying with or soon after having a cold. People who are outside the world of aviation will not be aware of the dangers of this, as colds are so commonplace and are such relatively minor ailments, but the resulting damage can be extremely serious and sometimes permanent. You will find that people will frequently want to book a trial flight for someone and they will ask you 'He suffers from "condition X" – is that a problem?' More often than not you won't know the answer to that straight away, unless it happens to be something you have come across in the past, so the best thing to do is take their phone number and speak to the CFI to see if they have any ideas. Ultimately, however, if you are going to be taking this person flying then as captain they will be your responsibility, so if you're not happy with anything, say so.

ON THE DAY

Weather
At the start of a day when you have trial lessons booked in, your priority should be to check the weather. You need to be able to make a decision about the suitability of the weather as early as possible where trial lessons are concerned because often they will telephone first thing in the morning to check whether their flight is going ahead, even if they are not scheduled to fly until much later in the day. The reason for this is sometimes just the fact that they have a long distance to travel, but often it is because they are setting off hours in advance in order to pick up friends and family members at various points along the way. If the weather is fine there is no problem, but if it is unsuitable then it is definitely worth calling any trial lesson customers who have not already contacted you before they start to make their way to the airfield, otherwise you can guarantee that they will forget to call the flying school and will just turn up.

If the weather forecast is ambiguous, you can make a decision for your early bookings based on what the weather looks like it is doing now, at your home airfield and any local airfields that can give you an actual. In terms of your later bookings, however, you really need to delay making a decision until you have had chance to see the later, and hence more accurate, forecasts (*see* Useful Information for TAF issue times). To give your trial lessons the best chance of going ahead, therefore, it is a good idea to speak to the customers to briefly explain this situation: ask them if they could call you back for a decision as late as possible, just before they are about to leave, when you will have the very latest information available to you.

Many trial lesson customers will elect to drive down to the airfield anyway, regardless of whether their flight is going ahead or not. This is usually because they are interested in learning to fly and want to have a look around and a chat even if they don't get airborne, or sometimes if the trial lesson had been a major event for someone with lots of friends and family coming along to watch, they will decide to carry on with their plans, stay for a drink and a look at the aircraft, and then re-schedule their trip for another day.

On the subject of trial lessons and the weather, you may occasionally come across someone who really wants their flight to go ahead even if the weather is not ideal, most commonly if, as in the above example, it is a big occasion with their family and friends having had time off work and so on, to watch. There is a big difference between the weather being not ideally suitable and it being totally unfit to fly, so if you are happy that the weather is in fact fit to fly – albeit not ideally suitable – then there is no reason not to take them. So long as you have explained to them that they will not be able to see very much (or whatever the problem with the weather is) and they accept that, then it is their decision.

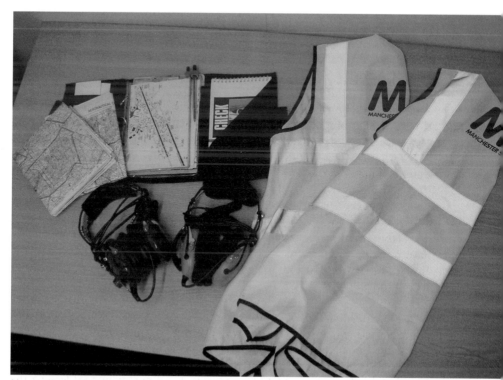

Have all your equipment ready.

Prepare the Aircraft

When you are preparing the aircraft for taking trial lessons, there are a few items to include in your checklist in addition to your normal walkround and pre-flight preparations. Primarily, your aim is to minimize the inevitable confusion that occurs – and therefore the time that is wasted at the start of each flight – when you are dealing with people who are unlikely to have ever been in a light aircraft before. Tactics for this can include having all the headsets already plugged in with wires tucked away so feet don't become tangled in them (if your apron is secure enough to leave them unattended), and seatbelts untangled and laid out neatly in advance, before any people even arrive on the scene. It is also beneficial to have all your own bits and pieces such as headset, kneeboard, chart and pens ready, so that you don't add to the confusion yourself by forgetting something and having to go back for it.

You should check all the aircraft seat pockets and side pockets for airsickness bags and ensure that there are three or four bags in each pocket. These should be placed discreetly, so that people can see they are there, but so that they are not too glaringly obvious. You should also make sure you have a stash of three or four in your kneeboard for speedy access if necessary, so that there is one to hand wherever you are seated in the aircraft, at a moment's notice.

As mentioned earlier, it is also a good idea to take this opportunity before people arrive to keep the aircraft cool. If it is cloudy or raining then the aircraft should remain fairly cool anyway, but on a sunny day it can become extremely hot inside the aircraft when it is parked up, so it is worth opening the doors and DV window to keep it as cool as possible in preparation for your flight. You should also show your trial lesson occupants how to operate the air vents before they climb in. Even though these vents should remain closed until after start-up, they should be opened as soon as possible afterwards, and it can be difficult trying to explain how to work them once people are seated in the aircraft.

Admittedly this may not be the best idea on a freezing cold day, but even when it is slightly warm outside, your aircraft is likely to become hot and stuffy, which in turn could be unpleasant for your customer. Far better to start off cool and then close the vents or put the heater on, rather than quickly become too hot and then not be able to do anything about it.

All these are simple tasks, but to people who are unfamiliar with light aircraft they can be quite time-consuming; it is far better to spend a few minutes doing these things yourself before your customer arrives, rather than trying to do them when you have an aircraft full of people.

Another useful thing to do when preparing the aircraft is to make sure that there are cushions readily available. This is in case your customer has difficulty in seeing over the coaming – a common problem with aircraft such as the Piper Cherokee – because you cannot even try to conduct a lesson if your student can't see out. There are usually a handful of cushions in existence at a flying school and when not in use these may be kept in a store cupboard or, more likely, just left in the back of the aircraft in which they were last used. It is essential that you locate the cushions early, before all the aircraft start to go flying, because it can cause a real problem if you suddenly realize that you need a cushion and then discover they are all airborne in the back of the other aircraft.

There will normally be plenty of cushions to go around as it is unlikely that more than one or two people will need them at any one time, so the best thing to do is to retrieve any that you find in the back of aircraft and take them all into the flying school building. That way, you know you have got access to cushions if you need them, plus you know that you are not taking them all flying with you if somebody else needs them.

When They Arrive

When your customer arrives they are likely to be accompanied by a crowd of supporters. They will normally be nervous, excitable and looking forward to their potentially once-in-a-lifetime experience. From the moment you are introduced as their instructor you should make a conscious effort to be as welcoming and as enthusiastic as you can, even when this is your sixth trial lesson of the day and you really just want to go home. To your customer, you are the face of the flying school and they will be concentrating on everything you say, absorbing every moment of their experience. It is often as important a day for their friends and family (who have probably clubbed together to pay for the flight) as it is for the person themselves, so try to make it special for them too, involving them in the briefing if possible and allowing them to take photographs of the aircraft. Remember that every single trial lesson customer you fly with is a potential new student for you, so it is in your interests to do your very best with each and every one.

Complete the Paperwork

At every flying school there will be some sort of 'Temporary Membership' or 'Trial Lesson Membership' form that customers will need to fill in before they can fly. The form will ask for details such as the person's name and address, date of birth and their signature, or the signature of a parent or guardian for those under the age of eighteen, and the purpose of the form is to effectively make the person a member of the flying school on the day that their flight is taking place. It is necessary to do this in order for them to be covered on the school's insurance policies and it is therefore of great importance that they should complete one of these forms prior to their flight.

When a trial lesson customer arrives at the flying school, the ops staff will usually identify their booking on the flying programme, take the person's trial lesson voucher off them and then immediately ask them to fill in one of the temporary membership forms so that it is done and out of the way. Occasionally, however, this might be missed, so it is always worth asking your customer whether they have filled in a form before you walk out to the aircraft and, if not, ask them to do so there and then. If they have not

Ensure that trial lesson customers complete the relevant paperwork.

completed the appropriate form then the chances are that they have not yet handed in their voucher either, so at this point you should ask them for that, too. Ops need the vouchers to be surrendered on the day the flight is taken so that they can keep track of the lessons flown out of all those purchased, whilst also preventing the possibility of the voucher being used again at a later date.

Awkward Surprises

Having now met your customer and had a look at them, you may occasionally find yourself in the awkward position that you believe there may be a problem with their weight or size, with respect to the aircraft you are scheduled to take them flying in. As discussed previously, these factors should have been mentioned at the time they bought the trial lesson but occasionally – and inevitably – people will slip through the net. As captain you have the ultimate responsibility for the safety of the flight so, as embarrassing and awkward as it is discussing these very personal issues with people (especially women), it is vital that you do so, for everyone's sake.

Weight and Size

If you are concerned that there may be a problem with excessive weight, you will need to weigh your customer to find their actual weight, rather than taking their word for it. Most flying schools will have some bathroom scales available for this exact purpose, so make sure you know where these are kept – ideally in another room – and discreetly ask your customer to come with you for a moment. Try to make as little fuss as possible, making them aware that it is a perfectly routine exercise, and then tell them you just need a minute to do your pre-flight calculations.

It may be that your customer is within the weight limit for the aircraft, but is physically very large. Some light aircraft seatbelts are sufficiently extendable for most people, but others are very restrictive. There should always be at least one extension seatbelt available at your flying school for such an eventuality (and if not, they really need to buy one), so familiarize yourself with how to use it and know where it lives, just in case. It will be up to you to avoid an embarrassing moment, again acting discreetly and without fuss to avoid drawing unnecessary attention to the situation.

When faced with these types of problems there will often be a quick and painless solution, because either your weight and balance calculation will show that you are within limits, or your extension seatbelt will do the job admirably, so that you can carry on with your flight as planned. If not, however, there is very little you can do; you would be left with no choice but to either de-fuel the aircraft you were meant to be taking or to change to a larger aircraft, if one is available. Obviously the specific circumstances of your situation will dictate what happens, such as whether your flying school actually has a larger aircraft – it may not, in which case you really will be stuck – but it is always going to be awkward. The only way to avoid such unpleasant occurrences is to make sure all the right questions are asked in the first place.

Physical problems

On occasion you may be presented with a person who looks like they may not be physically able to climb into the aircraft. Most people don't know what aeroplanes are really like and assume that they are very much like cars to get into and out of, so they may not have even considered it to be an issue.

Think about Piper and Cessna aircraft as two examples with which a huge number of flying schools are equipped. To climb into a Piper Tomahawk or Cherokee, your customer must lift their foot quite high up to reach the wing, and hoist themselves up until they are standing on it, then lower themselves down into the seat, often with their legs and feet all over the place. To climb into a Cessna it is again a high step up either onto an intermediate step or into the cabin itself, another hoist of their body to slide themselves in and another entanglement of limbs to organize before they are sitting correctly in the seat. For a younger person this can usually be achieved without hesitation, but for an older or less agile person it can be a major obstacle, sometimes to the extent that they cannot climb in at all.

When the trial lesson had been booked, if they had said the flight was for someone quite elderly then this potential problem should have been drawn to their attention. Sometimes a member of the family will come along to the flying school in advance, purely to see if they think the person would be able to manage getting in and out, before booking the person a flight. Often, however, the situation does not become apparent until the day itself and at this point you will have to deal with it. More often than not a person will be able to get into and out of the aircraft if they are assisted by someone else, usually one of the family members who have come along to watch.

The only thing to bear in mind in this situation is what would happen in the case of an emergency evacuation: you could not be expected, or may not be able, to hoist the person out yourself, but if you are satisfied that they would not hinder your own escape from the aircraft, and they accept the situation, there is no reason not to proceed with the flight as planned.

Miscellaneous problems

You may sometimes be presented with an unusual situation, such as someone who is drunk when they arrive for their trial lesson. As many trial lessons are given as birthday gifts the person will often have been taken out for lunch beforehand, and although most people guess that it is a good idea to abstain from a birthday pint (or ten) until after their flight, there will always be the one who does not. In terms of legalities, it is illegal to be drunk whilst on board an aircraft. Remember, however, that the effect of even a small amount of alcohol can be exaggerated at altitude, and you have no way of knowing how the person is going to react once you are up there. As captain of the aircraft, the decision of whether you are prepared to take them flying ultimately lies with you. If in doubt, see if they could come back in a few hours or on another day. If they don't like it, they should have used a little more common sense and thought about that beforehand!

Another example of an unusual situation is that of a woman who is pregnant, either having the trial lesson herself or wanting to fly in the back as an observer. As a guide, a woman can fly as a pilot (although multi-crew only) up to twenty-six weeks of pregnancy, assuming that the pregnancy is progressing with no complications as assessed by her GP or midwife, but even then it is impossible to make general statements on this subject because each specific case will be different. All you could do would be to make the woman aware that she was flying at her own risk, making her aware of the physical sensations involved in flying in a light aircraft, and that as a single-pilot operation you would be unable to provide any assistance to her if anything happened during the flight. Ultimately, however, it would be entirely your decision whether to agree to take her flying or not.

WHAT DO THEY WISH TO ACHIEVE?

Having now greeted your customer, checked that they have completed the relevant paperwork and not noted any obvious problems, you now need to have a brief chat with them to find out the basics of their background and what they personally want to achieve from their trial lesson. This will take a matter of moments but will give you a clear picture in your own mind of how to conduct the lesson overall, of any points that you particularly need to focus on and of how much detail to go into at each stage of the flight.

The first question to ask is whether the person is actually interested in learning to fly. You should then ask whether or not they have ever previously flown in a light aircraft, primarily because this will tell you whether they know what physical sensations to expect once you are airborne, but also to give you an idea of their background: if they say they have never flown in a light aircraft before you know that you are dealing with a complete novice, whereas if they have done some flying in the past then the whole experience will be more familiar to them. Whatever their level of previous flying experience, you should now be able to pitch the lesson according to their own particular circumstances, to give them the most from their flight.

Having sorted out all that, you now need to make sure that your customer has been to the toilet and has got their camera, because everyone always wants to do these two things and a lot of time can be wasted walking to and from the aircraft on the apron if they are forgotten. Also, many trial lesson customers will want to have their photograph taken standing with the aircraft or seated inside the aircraft before you go, a task usually undertaken by their accompanying family or friends.

Whether or not this takes place will be largely determined by the rules at your airfield for people who are not themselves flying wandering around airside. Usually there is somewhere for viewers to stand and watch people who are having a flight, and often the rules will allow one or two people airside to walk over to the aircraft with you, as long as it is safe for them to walk back again (such as not crossing an active taxiway). Ultimately, however, it is up to you, and if you are running late or everyone wants to come over, it may be simpler just to ask them all to stay landside and offer to take a couple of photographs of the person in the aircraft yourself.

One-Off Experience
If the person is having their trial lesson as a one-off experience (such as a birthday present) with no specific interest in learning to fly, it is important to prioritise their enjoyment of the flight over baffling them with information.

1. Find out where they live
Everybody loves to see their house from the air, so it is great to make a point of going to find it if at all possible. It is likely that when you ask where they live it may be somewhere that you have never even heard of. If this is the case

Find out where your trial lesson customer lives before setting off.

you may have difficulty in pinpointing the exact location on your aeronautical chart, so it is a good idea to have a road map handy and to ask the person to show you where their house is before you set off. That way you can transfer the location on to your chart either mentally, or physically with a map marker, plus you will then be able to organize your routing for the rest of the flight accordingly. Heading off in a particular direction should not be a problem, because although flying schools tend to have designated 'routes' for their trial lessons you should be able to go wherever you want, assuming that the airspace and your allocated time for the flight will allow it.

2. Give a brief brief

All that the brief needs to consist of is the basics of the attitude for straight and level, the primary flying controls and their effects, and the basic instruments. Don't go into unnecessary detail, and remember that the person is likely to be so excited and nervous that they won't take much of it in anyway.

74

3. Limit the information you provide to the basics

Once in the aircraft, the person will usually be quite overwhelmed by the whole experience. Get them strapped in, give them the necessary emergency brief, and then let them sit back and enjoy it. You very much have to tailor each flight to the individual person, because some people will want to know all about what you are doing in terms of the radio and your checks, whilst others will prefer just to watch. It is good to give a general commentary of what you are doing, without going into detail (such as, for the power checks, 'I'm now going to do the checks that we carry out before every flight'), but there is certainly no need to explain everything, unless they specifically ask.

This also applies once you are airborne, as some people will be very interested in what you are doing and will ask lots of questions, whilst others will want to quietly admire the view. Likewise, some people will be very eager to get their hands on the controls and want to fly the aircraft for the whole trip, whilst others will prefer to leave you to do the flying so they can just watch and absorb the experience.

Whatever the circumstances, however, always demonstrate the basic effects of controls as discussed in the brief and offer the person control of the aircraft, so that it is definitely a 'trial lesson' and not a 'pleasure flight', but whether they choose to fly it or not is entirely up to them. On this subject, it is important not to assume that somebody is not interested just because they are quiet. Flying in a light aircraft, particularly for the first time, can be a totally overwhelming experience for many people so do keep your commentary going: refer them to where they are, to visible landmarks and to well-known features to maintain their interest. You can also keep them informed about the basics of what you are doing, such as speaking to ATC or carrying out a FREDA check, to help them feel reassured. It is worth remembering that somebody who has never even considered learning to fly but who is bought a trial lesson as a one-off gift may suddenly fall in love with it and want to get a licence, so it is up to you to make them enjoy the experience as much as you can.

Interested in Learning to Fly

If the person is having their trial lesson with a view to learning to fly, you can provide them with more detailed information throughout the lesson as they are likely to be keen to learn and ready to absorb it all. That said, it will still often be their first experience of flying in a light aircraft, so it is important not to overwhelm them with too much information, or they may have so much to take in that they feel out of their depth.

1. Still give a fairly brief brief

You do not want to overload the person with information before you have even walked out to the aircraft, so still keep your brief to the basics. You can then elaborate on the points made in the brief once you are airborne, if and when you feel that they can absorb it. Also, even when someone is seriously

Try to make your customer feel at home in the aircraft.

considering learning to fly they will be excited to see their house from the air, so sort that out on the ground prior to walking out, as before.

2. Provide information steadily throughout the flight

When you first climb into the aircraft it is likely that the person will feel slightly overwhelmed, so only tell them what is necessary to begin with. As they are considering learning to fly you need to make them feel at home in the aircraft as quickly as possible: they will probably feel as though they couldn't possibly ever fly one of these things themselves with so much to look at and understand, and they may even feel slightly demoralized by this at first. It is therefore up to you to reassure them that everybody feels like this on their first flight, so not to be put off by it, but to enjoy themselves.

As you progress through your checks and radio calls it is beneficial to very briefly say what you are doing, in order to make the person feel part of it, but vital not to explain everything because there is far too much to take in all at once and they may start to feel put off again. Once airborne, the person is likely to be keen to take control of the aircraft, although even the keenest of people are often a little dubious about taking control at first –

not so much about them taking control, but about you letting go of the controls! After a few minutes, however, they usually settle into it and enjoy themselves, and you can then judge each person individually. Sometimes the person is keen to see as much as possible on their trial lesson so you can show them an introduction to several exercises, such as the basics of straight and level, climbing and descending and turning, whereas on other occasions they will be happy to fly the aircraft round without going into too much detail.

It may be that they are interested in being shown what a specific item does, such as the flaps or a GPS, in which case you could concentrate on this for a few minutes. I have even done a few circuits with people on trial lessons, when circumstances have allowed, which really gives them a taste of what learning to fly involves; if you operate from a flexible airfield in flexible airspace, the possibilities are endless. Ultimately though, the purpose of the flight is for them to experience being airborne and controlling a light aircraft, so you should aim to provide as much or as little information as they seem to want. If they go away feeling good about their progress and that they have learnt something, it will really inspire them to come back.

QUIETNESS

No matter how interested in flying someone is, they will often sit there next to you in complete silence for the majority of the flight. Some people will ask plenty of questions but many will not utter a single word. This is hardly surprising, considering that the whole environment with its unique sights, sounds and sensations will usually be totally unfamiliar to them, or often it can just be the fact that people feel self-conscious when they can hear their own voice in their headset. The situation can make life quite difficult for you, however, as it is your job to keep some sort of conversation going, to avoid an hour's worth of awkward silence.

Having talked about the aircraft's controls and instruments for a few minutes, then having allowed the person to take control and talked about that for a few more, you can sometimes run out of things to say altogether – and you may still have thirty minutes of the flight left to go! Worse still, it may be a two-hour trial lesson where you will really be struggling to think of vaguely interesting things to say for all that time. Here, then, are some ideas to help prevent any moments of awkwardness if you are getting desperate.

- Talk about what you are saying over the R/T, in basic language.
- Talk about airspace, showing how close you are to your airfield and to other local airfields on the map. People are usually amazed, and sometimes horrified, to discover that aeroplanes often fly around without being 'controlled' by anybody, with the pilots just using their eyes to look out for other aircraft coming the other way.

- Talk about some of the aircraft's other kit, such as the transponder or radio aids, keeping it simple.
- Talk about the weather! Something as simple as the cloud formations you can see, the visibility, and the colours of the sky can all provide a few moments of conversation.
- Talk about where you are: the towns, railway lines, motorways, and distinctive features such as hills, mountains, coastlines or lakes that are visible. Orientate this with regard to other visible places, highlighting how far you can see, and show the person this on your map. Also point out any well-known landmarks such as castles, bridges or stately homes.
- Chat about the landscape in general: all the different colours of the fields, how large or small the towns appear to be and how different everything looks from the air – point out the fact that even places that you know very well on the ground can look totally unrecognizable from the air, until you become used to what to look for.

If you intersperse conversation with FREDA checks and R/T calls you should be able to keep your customer entertained for the whole time, even if they prefer to just sit and listen. By the time you are routing back towards the airfield for landing, you can point out the roads they would have driven along to get there, then the airfield itself once it becomes visible. You can mention the way that you will be rejoining to fit in with any other traffic; after that they will see that you are busy with your checks, so they won't expect any further commentary anyway.

The main point to remember with quiet trial lesson customers is not to allow their quietness to make you feel uncomfortable. It is very easy to worry that they are not enjoying themselves, that they are not interested, or are just bored, but this is rarely the case. On one occasion in particular I took the landlord of a local pub for a trial lesson. He had expressed an interest in learning to fly but once airborne did not utter a single word, and I thought he must have been hating it as we flew around for an hour, largely in silence. The only time he did speak was five minutes before we landed, when to my surprise he suddenly said 'There's my pub.' I was sure we would not see him again, but a week later he signed up for a PPL course, then went on to complete a CPL, and is now a flying instructor himself. Enough said.

Chapter 5
The Flying
Course

During the Flight Instructor Course (FIC) you will have spent a great deal of time looking in detail at each individual lesson in the PPL syllabus, including the theory behind each lesson in the form of long and short briefings, and the content of each airborne lesson itself. This chapter is not a repeat of that information, but merely some additional points to think about: those which apply throughout the whole of the flight training course are looked at first, and others which are specific to individual exercises are looked at later on in the chapter. It should be noted that when referring to specific exercises, these apply equally to both the JAR PPL and the NPPL syllabus.

OVERALL POINTS

Length of Lessons

The length of each lesson that you deliver will vary significantly depending on the particular exercise you are teaching – an exercise such as turning may only last fifty minutes whereas a qualifying cross-country could last all day. Where a student is early on in their training, however, it is important to keep their lessons fairly short. Quite often, new students will ask for longer slots in order to cover the syllabus more speedily, but taking off and flying around for two or three hours in this situation rarely achieves the desired effect. Early on in a student's training when the aircraft environment – with all its unique sights, sounds, smells and sensations – is still so unfamiliar, they use up so much energy and concentration in trying to keep track of it all that they can really only absorb new information for an hour or so. If they do wish to fly for longer there is no reason why not, but by far the best option is to land and have a break and then go again, allowing the first block of information to sink in before starting again with the next block.

You could achieve this by booking two consecutive slots with your student (with just time for a quick break in between) or better still, if they have the time, book two slots in the same day separated by a couple of hours. This means that the student can have a drink, something to eat, think about what they did on their first lesson and prepare themselves for their second lesson before flying again. As this provides such excellent continuity (without being overwhelming) the student is likely to progress at the fastest possible rate, and from your point of view it can be very satisfying as you should see real progress by the end of the student's second flight of the day.

By the time a student is familiar with the environment later on in the flying course, their lessons will often be longer anyway (such as during circuit training or navigation), but even at this stage you should be ready to cut a lesson short if the student seems fatigued or overwhelmed with information. They may just be tired or 'having a bad day', but there is no point continuing with a lesson just for the sake of it – far better to save their money until next time when they are in a better frame of mind.

Order of Lessons

The syllabus is laid out in a particular order so that students who are learning to fly can progress through their training in a methodical manner, and it is therefore preferable to follow this order of training wherever possible. There will, however, be times when you will be forced to re-think the order of lessons you are due to give, either because of factors concerning the progress of the student whose lesson it is, or concerning the weather on the day.

According to the syllabus of flight exercises, a student should be taught a specific list of facts during a lesson that lasts a specific length of time, and after this lesson they will have learnt these facts and will be able to handle the aircraft to the required standard for the exercise. Sometimes this is exactly what does happen, but on many occasions the student will not have learnt how to fly the exercise properly and thoroughly within the timescale of the lesson.

If a student is struggling with an aspect of, or all of, a particular exercise, then it is pointless moving on to the next exercise until they have mastered it. Progressing on to the next exercise will only leave the student even more confused and frustrated, and this in itself will serve to hinder their progress further still. It is far better to re-visit the same exercise on the student's next lesson after they have had some time to think about it, as this will enable them to consolidate and then build upon what they learnt last time, and hopefully to reach an acceptable standard. Sometimes, if a student is told that they will be covering the same exercise again on their next lesson they will become concerned about their ability to fly at all. It is, however, a perfectly normal situation to be in, as most people encounter some sort of difficulty at some stage during their flight training, so you should reassure them that this is the case and not to worry.

There will be many occasions when the weather is unsuitable for the lesson you had planned to give, but perfectly good enough for other exercises. A frequent example of this is when a student is due to be taught climbing and descending, and although the visibility is good and there is no wind, the cloudbase is only 1,500ft. It would be a waste of time trying to achieve the lesson in these circumstances – so what do you do? It would be a great pity not to take advantage of it being a good day to fly, albeit not for climbing and descending, so do something else instead. Obviously at this early stage of your student's training you would be fairly limited in your choices of suitable alternatives, but there is a certain amount of flexibility where the actual order of lessons is concerned, whilst still being of benefit to the student.

There is no guidance published in the syllabus in terms of which lesson would be suitable as a substitute for another, so it is just a case of using common sense: think about which exercises the student has already completed, and therefore what they are already familiar with, and choose an alternative lesson which will only introduce a small amount of new information. For example, a student who has only got as far as straight and level would gain nothing from a lesson on radio navigation; they will still be unfamiliar with the aircraft environment and will only be able to absorb a small quantity of new information on each flight, so this would be too big a jump. A student who has completed straight and level, climbing, descending and turning, however, should be quite capable of absorbing a lesson on basic instrument flying; by this stage they will be far more familiar with flying generally, and they have learned the basic skills required to carry out this lesson – flying the aircraft straight and level, climbing, descending and turning – so the only difference is that this time it would be under simulated instrument conditions.

Sometimes if a student is told that they are moving on to a later exercise they are concerned about their ability to complete it, and unsure whether it will be of any benefit to them in the long term. You can reassure them, however, that it is quite normal practice in certain circumstances (usually weather-related), and so long as you use your knowledge of the particular student's ability and your common sense in choosing a suitable alternative lesson, they should gain as much from it as they would have done from the lesson that had originally been planned. Certainly in most cases, it is more beneficial for the student to maintain their continuity of flying (even if this means having to be taught an alternative lesson) than to leave it until a day which is suitable for the next lesson in the syllabus, resulting in them not flying for a month.

Rear-Seat Observers

Students will sometimes ask if it is acceptable to bring someone with them on their next lesson to sit in the back and watch, and this can be whether they are learning in four-seater aircraft, or are choosing to take a four-seater aircraft for their next lesson specifically for this reason. Your flying school may or may not have their own views and policies on this, but assuming that the person can be classed as a genuinely 'interested observer' to the person having the lesson, such as a spouse, parent, or suchlike, rather than just as a 'passenger', and that they are not specifically paying for their seat on the flight as a passenger would, then there is no reason why it should not go ahead. Your main concern in this type of situation is that you do not carry paying 'passengers' on a flight, so that it could be seen as a 'pleasure flight' rather than purely a training flight (or you could find yourself in serious trouble with the CAA!).

There are certain practicalities to think about when considering taking an extra person in the back of the aircraft on a lesson. The most obvious point is that if the student normally flies a two-seater aircraft and wishes to take a four-seater aircraft on this occasion, they must accept that their progress will be hindered by having to adapt to a different aircraft type. Secondly, even if the four-seater aircraft is the type that they usually fly, it should be pointed out to your student that the aircraft will handle differently, to a greater or lesser extent depending on type, and that this in itself could affect their progress; if they are having to spend the whole lesson trying to adjust the trim correctly, they may not progress through the exercise as successfully as they otherwise would have done. Finally, the 'interested observer' can potentially act as a distraction to the lesson, especially if they insist on talking and asking lots of questions – or being sick! Whilst the former can be avoided by turning down the rear intercom, or unplugging their headset altogether, there is little that can be done about the latter!

There are also certain exercises which common sense dictates are more appropriate for taking rear-seat observers than others (such as not taking your student's ageing relative on a particularly vicious stalling detail). This factor should also be discussed with the student before a decision is made, as it may necessitate carrying out a different lesson to the one which had been planned. If you are satisfied that the lesson is suitable, however, and that you have raised the above points, your student can make an informed choice about whether to go ahead or not. Ultimately it is their money, so if you have made your student fully aware of the implications of taking someone in the back, and you are personally happy to do so in the circumstances, then it is their decision.

Briefings

A pre-flight briefing is an essential part of each and every lesson. The purpose of a briefing is both to enable the instructor to set out what is to be taught, and to enable the student to see what will be expected of them during their lesson. It is an opportunity to revise important points from previous lessons and relate these to what is being covered today, whilst reinforcing principles that apply across every lesson to help the student remember them. Throughout the briefing there will inevitably be questions raised by the student and you should try to answer these as clearly as you can, without going into too much lengthy detail: you want your student to understand what is going on during their lesson, but don't want them to have expended all their brain power before you have even got airborne. It should also be remembered that a simple demonstration in the air can be as valuable as many minutes of explanation on the ground, so if your student is struggling to grasp a particular aspect of the briefing it might be more useful to actually show them what you mean once you are airborne, rather than bombard them with theory on the ground.

During the Flight Instructor Course you will have covered the long brief and short brief for every exercise in the flying syllabus, but in practice there is

A pre-flight briefing is essential.

usually only time to work through the short (or 'pre-flight') brief with a student before their lesson. The long brief contains a far greater depth of information, so it is very useful to have worked through it with your student at some point prior to their lesson. However, as with all these things, the opportunity to do so will often not arise; it would usually necessitate the student coming along to the flying school on an entirely separate occasion, specifically for that purpose, which is often not possible. The content of the long brief is only the same as the content of the student's textbook, however, so this emphasizes how important it is for your student to read up the appropriate section of their book prior to the time of their lesson, so that your pre-flight brief is familiar to them, merely revising the information that they have already read.

De-Briefings

A de-brief after a flight is equally as important as a pre-flight brief before a flight. It enables you and the student to review what happened during the lesson, what went well, what caused difficulties, how these could be overcome on subsequent flights, and what to think about for their next lesson. It should be seen by the student as an opportunity to get everything clear in their mind about what they have learnt before going home, but also to be able to ask questions about anything they are unsure of without feeling embarrassed. I have sometimes overheard an instructor giving a debriefing and have wondered if their poor student will ever come back to fly again: some instructors seem to have the idea that a 'debriefing' should omit to mention anything the student might have done correctly and should purely focus on the bad points, the things the student did wrong or forgot to do altogether.

Indeed, students will frequently do things wrong and will forget to do things, but surely it is the job of their instructor to teach them and to provide guidance on how to do it properly in the future – not to make them feel utterly useless and to wish they had never set foot in an aeroplane in the first place. It is of course essential to point out the student's mistakes, as they need to identify their mistakes in order to learn from them, but this should be dealt with in a constructive manner, such as by explaining how their performance could be improved upon next time. It is also important to highlight the good points, the things that the student did remember to do and aspects of the lesson that they achieved successfully, so that they can go away feeling positive about their experience and eager to come back for more.

Radiotelephony

Formal training and testing for the R/T licence is normally undertaken at a series of weekend or evening classes, and is an entirely separate entity from the remainder of the flight and ground training. To give your students practical experience of using the radio, however, it is a good idea to introduce it as part of their lessons from an early stage in their training. Initially you should limit their use of R/T to very simple messages whilst you are still on the ground – so they are not trying to fly and speak at the same time – and build this up progressively as they become more confident and familiar with it. You can explain the basic details of the phrases to be used and what will be said, discussing it as part of the pre-flight brief, and have some guidance notes for them to refer to once you are in the aircraft to take care of the inevitable 'mental block' that occurs as soon as the PTT is pressed!

As the student progresses in their flight training they can also progress in their use of the R/T, again with the assistance of guidance notes if necessary. Having used R/T in real situations during their lessons, your students will certainly be much better prepared for their R/T course and for passing both the written and practical R/T examinations.

Airmanship

Airmanship points form part of every pre-flight briefing, and throughout your Flight Instructor Course you will have been shown and will have worked through these for every flight exercise in the syllabus. In practice, instructors do indeed tend to mention these points to students during every pre-flight briefing, but it is essential to really emphasize how important they are in their own right. From a student's very first lesson they are working towards ultimately becoming the commander of an aircraft, and as their instructor you are responsible for developing every aspect of their skills, equipping them with the knowledge and abilities to achieve this. Whilst much of this knowledge and ability is in the direct form of being able to competently handle the aircraft, a large part is in the form of having good situational awareness and judgement, and using these skills in order to make sensible and safe decisions as an aircraft captain.

Throughout each lesson that you deliver, therefore, it is important to reiterate the airmanship points raised in your briefing, relating them to their real-life applications during a flight. If you are looking out and you see another aircraft, for example, highlight this fact to your student, making reference to its position in terms of the 'clock code' discussed in your briefing. If you are demonstrating the use of flaps, emphasize your check of the airspeed being 'below V_{FE}' and relate this statement to the white arc on the airspeed indicator, as discussed in your briefing. It is only by seeing airmanship points occurring during the course of a real flight that a student will recognize their importance, and it is only through the repetition of these points that a student will gradually absorb and remember them.

In a similar manner, it is necessary to keep your students aware of the reasons why certain things are done during a flight, rather than just the fact that they are done. Of course it would be impractical to explain the reasons behind every action you perform throughout every single lesson, but where something specific has been talked about in the briefing and you are carrying it out during the flight, remind the student why you are doing it. Sometimes it will be best to mention this briefly at the time and to discuss it more thoroughly in the de-brief, but either way the outcome is the same: if your student understands why they need to do something, they are far more likely to remember to do it without being prompted next time, and thus will be able to make decisions about it for themselves in the future.

Groundschool

Some students who are studying for the written exams are quite happy to read their training manuals on each subject, perhaps noting down the odd query to clarify with their instructor, and then sit the exam. Other students prefer to have all the subjects for the written exams taught to them, either on a course with other students, or one-to-one with an instructor. Whilst some of the exam subjects are fairly straightforward to learn purely through self-study (such as Human Performance and Limitations), the more involved subjects (such as Navigation) are not, and normally do require a certain amount of input from an instructor. It makes no difference how each student chooses to study, however, and most people will use a combination of the two methods in order to pass their exams.

Many flying schools run evening or weekend groundschool courses on each subject in the ground-training syllabus, and all the instructors will usually have the opportunity to teach at least one of these groundschool courses if they want to. Some schools will have a complete set of ready-made course notes and study materials for each subject to use in these classes,

Some flying schools have structured groundschool courses.

although some will not, relying on the instructors themselves to put together the course material for the subject they are going to teach. Whatever the groundschool situation is at your flying school, you will undoubtedly find yourself giving one or more students a groundschool lesson at some point, and if this is being conducted as 'groundschool' as opposed to just as a briefing, it will normally be paid work. It is therefore essential that you always have with you the notes from your Flight Instructor Course plus a copy of the ground-training syllabus, so that you know how much depth to go into in each area.

Giving groundschool lectures to students has advantages for both the student and the instructor. It enables the student to focus exclusively on the task in hand (without all the distractions of trying to study at home, or during a break at work), enabling them to gain further explanation of anything they are unsure of there and then, rather than puzzling over it for hours in a book. It provides the instructor with an opportunity to revisit subjects that they may not have thought about for a long time, and therefore refreshes the information in their own mind.

If you have been asked to teach something that is very familiar to you then you should have no problem in delivering a lesson on it with minimal preparation time, but if it is something that does not come up very often in your day-to-day flying (such as the intricacies of the Chicago Convention, perhaps?) then you may not be quite so well equipped. For this reason, it is worth refreshing your own memory on the less-often-used areas of the ground syllabus on a regular basis, maybe even making some notes for yourself to refer to if necessary. If you are asked to teach a formal 'class' then you would have to be given sufficient time to prepare, but as many groundschool sessions are impromptu (usually only arising due to the weather being too bad to fly) you need to be in a position to set to work straight away so that you can make best use of the time available.

FLYING EXERCISES: GENERAL POINTS

Exercises 1 to 11

During the first few exercises a student will be experiencing both the environment and language of aviation, neither of which may have been experienced by them before. When everything is so unfamiliar it is essential that instructors do not overload students with too much information all at once, but instead deliver the information gradually, repeating and revising what has already been taught before moving on to the next stage.

There is a great deal of information to pass on to the student in these early exercises and much of this involves talking through things on the ground, such as an explanation of the tech log and aircraft documentation. These

Allow students to carry out the checks, under your supervision.

tasks are ideally suited to a day when the weather is unsuitable for flying as it brings the student into the flying school, thus keeping their interest and some continuity, and they will be in a relaxed frame of mind knowing they are not actually going flying; they will absorb the information far better by chatting through things over a cup of coffee, rather than trying to take it all in before or after a flight when they will be preoccupied with their actual lesson. It is also vital that during their first few visits all students read and sign the Flying Order Book, so that they are aware of the school's own rules and regulations.

It is beneficial to introduce a new student to the checks and other procedures a little at a time throughout their early lessons, perhaps talking them through how to do something – such as the walkround – on a couple of consecutive occasions before letting them have a go at it themselves. Their 'responsibilities' can then be gradually increased over each lesson to the point at which the student is happy to do everything (pre-flight checks, start-up, basic R/T, taxi, and so on.) with you just monitoring their actions.

Exercises 12 to 14
Having reached this stage in their training, a student should be competent at handling the aircraft on the ground and in the air, making R/T calls and having an understanding of airmanship issues, but until now their exact actions and the course of the flight will have been entirely dictated by you. The circuit is their first real opportunity to put all their new skills together and start to make decisions for themselves, and as their instructor it is very rewarding for you to see this in progress.

Some general points to instil into students during circuit training include an awareness of their position in relation to other aircraft in the circuit and the importance of utmost vigilance in ATZs, especially when it is busy. The student needs to be able to form a mental picture of where they are in relation to other traffic by using their eyes to look out and ears to listen out, but you should highlight to them that other aircraft may not actually be where they say they are, so they should never take this for granted. The student's judgement and decision-making skills will also be developed in the circuit, again in terms of other traffic such as correct positioning but also in terms of their handling of the aircraft, particularly where go-arounds and simulated emergencies are concerned. It is essential that your students learn to make these decisions for themselves, without the need to turn to you for confirmation, and this is a significant factor for you in judging their readiness for flying solo.

Exercise 18
(Exercises 15–17 are discussed later in this chapter.) Navigation is a vast subject that requires a large amount of time and preparation on the ground. The initial demonstration of how to thoroughly plan a navigation route is lengthy, as are the explanations of weight and balance calculations, performance calculations and radio navigation, so in an ideal situation these should be carried out on a day when the student is not actually flying –

otherwise they are likely to have reached mental saturation point before even climbing into the aircraft.

During the early navigation lessons, most students can either fly accurately or keep on top of everything that is going on, but not both. The ability to combine the skills of flying a specific height and heading whilst maintaining situational awareness, navigating and liaising with ATC only comes with practice, and the emphasis throughout navigation training should therefore be on the student learning to organize themselves appropriately and acting methodically in order to achieve this.

The preparation time needed for each navigation trip is longer than that required for other exercises, even when the student is quite experienced in navigation and has planned and studied the route in advance, and the student should be encouraged to develop their own thorough knowledge of what needs to be done in order to prepare for a navigation flight. Points deserving particular attention during navigation training are:

Pilot's log
Most students are equipped with an A5-size kneeboard and A5-size plog, but people sometimes struggle with these. If so, it may be helpful for them to try using a larger A4-size plog and kneeboard on their next flight to see if this is any better.

Overhead joins
The importance of carrying out overhead joins whenever possible cannot be stressed enough to students. Many an accident has almost occurred due to pilots joining 'straight in' on a leg of the circuit rather than joining overhead, and it is vital that students learn to position themselves correctly for an overhead join, as this in itself can be confusing if not practised regularly. The process does take an extra few minutes of your time, but it is most definitely worth it.

Making a note of the times
So often a student will return from a solo cross-country flight and will have not made a note of their brakes off/brakes on or airborne times. As an instructor it becomes a force of habit to write the times down, and you must therefore make a conscious effort to teach your students to write the times down for themselves; when they have just been for a short navigation flight it is not too difficult, but it is extremely time-consuming to find out from the various airfield ATC units what all their take-off and landing times were when they return from their qualifying cross-country, and their actual brakes off/brakes on times can only really be guesswork!

Replying to R/T calls
When students are immersed in a navigation trip they will frequently miss R/T calls from ATC. In these situations it is much easier to just give a reply

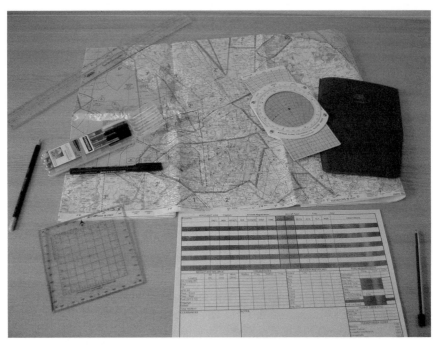

Use common sense when planning navigation routes.

yourself, and of course this is necessary when the student is early on in their navigation training. As they become more experienced, however, you must make an effort not to reply for them all the time, but leave them to it, even if ATC have to call a couple of times. It is necessary for the student to develop the ability to maintain a listening watch for their callsign, and they certainly need to have achieved this before they can undertake any solo navigation flights.

Along similar lines, warn them that they will not necessarily receive a reply when they call up on a frequency. If there is always a reply on the R/T at your home airfield it can be very disconcerting for the student if nobody replies to their calls, especially if they are solo, but at particular airfields the tower is only manned at weekends, whilst at other places there will sometimes be a reply and sometimes not. They should therefore be briefed on what to do in this situation so that they are prepared, rather than concerned, if this happens.

Planning routes the best way round
When deciding on routes to take and airfields to visit on navigation flights it is vital to take certain factors into consideration, especially when a student is to fly the trip solo. Where a route includes a predominantly south-westerly leg, for example, remember that flying into the sun can be very difficult on a hazy afternoon, so in these conditions consider flying the reciprocal of the route instead. Where a student is landing at other airfields (such as during a

qualifying cross-country) think about the order in which they should be visited; some airfields become unlicensed or close altogether earlier in the day than others, particularly in the winter months, so ensure the student is visiting the airfields the most sensible way round to give them the most time.

Exercises 15, 16, 17 and 19

These exercises can often be flown when the weather is unsuitable for the scheduled lesson, such as teaching Exercise 15 when there is too much cross-wind for circuits, or Exercise 19 when it is too hazy for navigation. Exercises 16 and 17 can also be useful in this way, although of course the student must be thoroughly proficient and experienced in these exercises before flying solo away from the circuit.

SKILL TEST: REVISION AND PREPARATION

Before a student can be put forward for a Skill Test they must have completed all their flight training and all their written exams. If you have a student who is approaching the point where they are ready for their Skill Test, therefore, you must ensure that these requirements have all been satisfied. The simplest way to do this whilst making sure that nothing has been omitted is to refer directly to the licence application form which can be obtained from the CAA website (*see* Useful Information for details). The licence application form contains full details of all the qualifying requirements for the issue of the licence it pertains to, be it the JAR-FCL PPL or NPPL. These include the exact number of dual flight training hours that must have been completed in both general handling and navigation, the exact number of solo flying hours that must have been completed in both general handling and navigation, the qualifying cross-country flight, the written exams that must have been passed and the medical certificate that must be held by the student applying for the licence. Only when all of the above criteria have been met can the student be submitted for their Skill Test.

Students are always very eager to add up their flying hours, particularly solo hours, and at any given moment can usually tell you how many hours they have logged to the nearest five minutes! People do not tend to keep such a careful track of their exam passes, however, and yet these are equally as important components of the licence they are training for. With this in mind, it is vital to keep track of not only your students' flying hours but also the actual dates on which they passed each of the written exams, as these must all be within the overall validity period in order for a Skill Test to be taken. If not, the exams are effectively incomplete, and therefore any Skill Test result would be void. The current rules state that all the written exams for the JAR PPL must be passed within an eighteen-month period, and thereafter are valid for licence issue for twenty-four months from the date of passing the last exam.

Another factor with the Skill Test is judging when to carry out the necessary revision prior to the Skill Test itself. When a student has reached the stage of being ready for their Skill Test, it is sensible to spend some time on the ground and in the air revising all the exercises that will be tested, many of which will not have been flown for several months. To prepare the student fully it is preferable to complete this revision as close as possible to the date scheduled for their Skill Test; there is little purpose in carrying out any revision flights much before this date, as the student will only have forgotten it all again by the time the date arrives.

As part of this revision it is beneficial to guide your student through all the ground work that will form an essential part of their Skill Test, such as fuel consumption, weight and balance, and performance calculations. These may also not have been looked at in detail for a while so it is important to refresh your student's memory, as they need to be confident in carrying out these important calculations under the scrutiny of an examiner.

Finally, always remember that your students will inevitably be very anxious about their Skill Test; for many people it is the final step towards achieving a lifetime's ambition, for others the first significant step towards their dream career. For everyone it is the cause of nerves, sometimes sleepless nights, and it is your job to provide as much assistance, guidance and support to your students as possible. Offer to spend some extra time with them going over any last-minute worries, or give them your telephone number so they can call you the night before if they think of something. Above all, recognize what an important occasion it is for them, as it had once been for you: provide reassurance to them if it does not go so well, but be sure to make a fuss and give them the congratulations they deserve if they pass.

CHAPTER 6
CHECKOUTS

The term 'checkout' tends to be used to refer to a flight taking place where the instructor is assessing and/or teaching someone who already holds a pilot's licence, and much of your time as a flying instructor will be taken up with checkouts. It would be reasonable to assume that – compared with your other flights, where you are flying with students or trial lessons – checking someone out who already holds a pilot's licence should be easy and straightforward. This, however, is rarely the case! There is an almost infinite number of scenarios surrounding pilots who come to you for checkouts and each of them will have vastly different levels of ability, despite the fact they already hold a licence. They will also want an array of different outcomes from their checkout, which you will need to know in order to plan a suitable course of training for them. Your primary task when faced with a checkout, therefore, is to find out as much information about the pilot as possible, so that you can decide upon a plan of action for them to follow in order to achieve their particular goal.

TYPES OF CHECKOUT

Currency
Each flying school will have its own rules regarding currency requirements for pilots hiring their aircraft. These rules will be clearly stated in the school's Flying Order Book (FOB) and every member of the school should have signed this document to say that they agree to abide by these rules. Most flying schools will have a currency period for their members of between four and six weeks, so that if a licence holder wishes to hire a school aircraft after this time has elapsed (since their last flight in the same aircraft type), they will be required to complete a checkout with an instructor first. There will also be specific currency rules regarding flights carried out at night, as night flying is very much a skill in its own right. Even though a pilot may have already flown an aircraft on a particular day, and be within their currency period to do so, they may not necessarily be within currency to fly that same aircraft once it has gone dark. Again, specific requirements for night currency will vary from school to school and these will all be stated in the FOB.

There are many variations to what is considered acceptable and what is not, where currency is concerned, such as if a licence holder had flown a particular aircraft type within the required currency period but from a different flying school. Each school will have their own set of rules to cater for different circumstances, and these may be stated in the FOB or may be at the discretion of the CFI in each individual case. You may also find that there are different 'levels' of checkout stated in your FOB, which require basic or more comprehensive revision depending on how far out of check the pilot is. For example, a basic checkout might apply to a pilot who is just outside a 28-day currency period, whereas a more comprehensive checkout would be required for a pilot who has not flown for six months. All this information will be contained within your FOB and this should be studied (photocopied for your file) and referred to where necessary.

Airfield/Aircraft Familiarization

Another occasion where a licence holder would need to be checked out by an instructor is if a new member of your school has previously flown the aircraft type operated by your school, but has never flown from your airfield before or, similarly, if a current member of your school wanted to convert from one aircraft type to another. Obviously, if they wished to fly a complex type, or add a new Class Rating or Type Rating to their licence, then a formal course of training must be undertaken and not merely a checkout. When familiarizing with a new airfield or converting to a new type within the same Class Rating, however (such as converting on to a Piper Archer from a Piper Tomahawk), then a checkout by one of the school's flying instructors would take place.

Pilots often convert from training aircraft to more advanced types.

This is a very common occurrence at flying schools, particularly in converting from two-seater aircraft to four-seater aircraft, but there is no standard laid down by the CAA for the training that should be undertaken. Where checkouts are to be completed under specific circumstances (such as when converting from the school's two-seater to the four-seater) then details of minimum training to be given may be stipulated in the school's FOB – but often they will not. You should, therefore, consult your CFI for guidance on a suitable course of training to provide individually in each case .

Rating Renewal/Revalidation

In addition to the rules stated by each individual flying school, there are also the overall rules regarding the currency of a licence holder's particular rating as stated by the CAA. As flying schools only tend to operate Single-Engine Piston (SEP) and Multi-Engine Piston (MEP) aircraft, the ratings that you will come across most frequently are SEP and MEP Class Ratings, in addition to the Simple Single-Engine Aeroplane (SSEA) Class Rating that is the SEP equivalent for NPPL holders. The requirements for the revalidation and renewal of these ratings are listed in Chapter Seven.

As far as currency is concerned, the only CAA rules relate to flights involving the carriage of passengers. In order to carry passengers, the holder of a SEP, MEP or SSEA Rating must have completed three take-offs and landings as sole manipulator of the flying controls within the preceding ninety days. If they are the holder of a night qualification and wish to carry passengers at night, at least one of the three take-offs and landings must have been completed at night. It should be noted that the definition is 'sole manipulator of the flying controls', rather than specifically 'solo' flight. It is therefore acceptable to fulfil the ninety-day requirement during the course of a 'dual' flight as long as the instructor does not take control at any point during the three take-offs and landings, by day, or one by night.

In terms of checkouts, you will often find yourself booked in with a licence holder to complete the 'dual flight' as part of their SEP or SSEA Class Rating revalidation. By its very definition of being a 'dual flight' this would normally mean that the pilot is 'under instruction'. In fact, it is intended that the instructor should merely assess the performance of the pilot, keeping their interjections to a minimum and only 'teaching' the pilot if they need assistance to reach the required standard, so it is more of a checkout than an instructional flight in these circumstances.

You will sometimes find that you are booked in with a licence holder for some revision prior to a renewal of their SEP or SSEA Class Rating. Their handling skills and overall ability will often be determined by how long it has been since they last flew (as it could potentially range from days to decades) and these revision flights will usually be a combination of both supervision and actual teaching until the pilot once again reaches the standard required of a Skill Test candidate. As the pilot does already hold a licence, however, such flights also tend to be referred to as checkouts.

Non-UK Licence Holders

The final type of checkout you are likely to encounter is where a non-UK licence holder wishes to fly in the UK, either on the strength of their own licence, or by converting their own licence to a UK licence. In terms of their ability as a pilot, your job will be just the same as with any other checkout (assessing their existing skills and teaching where necessary until they reach the required standard) but the paperwork can be significantly more complicated. This subject is discussed in Chapter Seven, and you should refer to the very latest information in the relevant AICs and LASORS, always seeking clarification from the CAA where necessary.

BACKGROUND INFORMATION

What are the Circumstances?

A pilot may need a checkout with an instructor because they have gone a few days over their flying school's currency period for hiring an aircraft. Another pilot may need a checkout because they have just moved to the UK from abroad where they held a non-UK PPL, and wish to convert to a UK PPL on an aircraft type that they have never flown before. As you can see, these are two totally different situations, which would need totally different preparation and input from the instructor. Often when you look through the booking sheets and see that you have a checkout booked in, it will just say 'checkout' and will give very little, if any, information about the person, their flying background, and what they want to achieve from their checkout. It is essential that you seek out this information prior to the day they are booked in to fly, because if it turns out to be complicated you may spend so long formulating a plan of what they need to do that you run out of time to fly at all.

Sometimes ops will ask a list of relevant questions at the time the person telephones or calls in to book their checkout, but this does not always happen and it will often be down to you to find it out for yourself. At a glance it does appear to be a barrage of questions, but the following list should cover the main points that you will need to know in order to prepare thoroughly for the person's flight.

- Do they have a current licence, and what type is it (NPPL/PPL/CPL/ATPL)?
- What is the expiry date of the rating that pertains to the aircraft they wish to fly?
- Do they have a current medical, and what is its expiry date?
- When did they last fly? What aircraft type? Where from?
- Have they flown from this airfield before? When was the last time (approximate)?
- Have they flown this aircraft type before? How many hours do they have on it (approximate)? When was the last time (approximate)?

- How many hours' total flying experience do they have?
- Do they hold any other ratings?

Obviously, both you and ops will recognize the names of people who fly from your school regularly, so there would be no need to interrogate them if you already knew all the answers – probably just clarification of the date they last flew. The questions should just be asked to people who are not familiar to you, and the reason for asking them is self-evident. For example, a pilot will need to spend a good deal of time on the ground going through the procedures in force at your airfield if they have never flown from there before, whereas one of your flying school's members who has just not flown for a while will know it all already, albeit being perhaps a little rusty. The questions about flying hours' logged and ratings held will help to give you a general overview of the person's experience, although this will not necessarily be a reflection of their ability on the day.

The questions about the ratings in their licence and medical details will also clarify to you – and to the person themselves – whether both these items are current, so you know whether or not you can send the person solo, and also whether you are working them towards a renewal. This seems far too obvious, but it is amazing how many times people will book themselves in for a six-week currency checkout, only to discover – when they arrive at the school and the instructor checks their licence – that their SEP Rating has lapsed. This immediately turns the basic revision lesson they were expecting into detailed preparation for a Skill Test instead. It is better for everyone to know what they are preparing for in advance, so by asking the questions you will minimize the chance of unexpected revelations on the day.

What is the Objective?
In terms of background information it is also important to be clear about what the person wants to achieve from their checkout. Some examples of this are:

- A current UK PPL holder visiting the area who wants to hire an aircraft for a few local trips, just throughout their stay.
- A JAR PPL holder whose licence has lapsed and who wants to revisit the basic exercises, but is not interested in actually renewing their licence.
- A current NPPL holder who has been flying elsewhere but now wants to fly from your school permanently.
- A current non-UK licence holder who wants to hire an aircraft from your school on the strength of their own licence.
- An airline captain who has not flown a single-engine aircraft for twenty years and who now wants to renew their SEP Rating.

Having obtained both the information about the person's flying details and about what they want to achieve from their checkout, you should now be equipped to tailor the time you have allocated with them to their exact needs, in pursuit of their personally desired outcome. Frequently, at this point in the conversation, people booking themselves in for a checkout will ask how long a slot they will need to complete it. Unfortunately, this is an impossible question to answer because you have no way of knowing how long it will take them to reach a satisfactory standard, irrespective of how recently they last flew or how long it took them on their last checkout. All you can do is to book them a slot and then see what happens on the day: either you will have covered everything and the checkout will be complete, or they will need to book in again for some more.

An uncomfortable situation can arise if someone has booked themselves in for an hour's checkout, having gone over their currency period, and has also booked the aircraft straight afterwards to take their friends for a flight. For them to assume that one hour's revision will be sufficient to meet the required standard is very naïve, and it is unfair of them to put an instructor in this situation at all.

This happened to me once, when the pilot had told ops he would only need a short checkout when he telephoned to book, and his friends had driven for over an hour to get to the airfield to fly with him in the next slot – but ops did not question it and I did not subsequently notice it. We started off with some circuits and his landings were very flat, in fact much too flat, and the whole hour consisted of me demonstrating good landings and him carrying out bad landings. There was no way he was going on his own after this first session, so he told his friends to go and amuse themselves whilst we went up again, in his second slot. After a while he did master the landings, but by then there was insufficient time to cover everything else, such as PFLs and stalling.

In the end, he and his friends had to come back the next day to finish off, and they did eventually manage to go for their flight, but if ops had highlighted to the man the possibility of this happening in the first place, he might have avoided the humiliation! This only goes to further reinforce the importance of keeping abreast of what ops have booked in for you and, if necessary, you or ops calling people back to express your concerns about the slots they have booked in.

STANDARDS

Regardless of the circumstances surrounding a checkout, they all have the same fundamental principal – to assess the pilot's existing skills and, where necessary, through revision and further training to bring these up to a satisfactory standard for the outcome that they want to achieve. There are very few pilots who can complete a checkout with an instructor and not struggle on a single exercise, either in the air or on the ground, so a small amount of revision and further training is usually required. Some people's overall performance will be very good and other people will make you wonder if they really do hold a licence at all, but either way it is your job to

Weight and balance calculations are an integral part of checkouts.

help them to achieve an acceptable standard on the ground and in the air. For example, most pilots on checkouts cannot carry out a satisfactory PFL first time, nor can most pilots on checkouts perform a weight and balance calculation correctly, and these are the two areas you will find yourself having to go through on virtually every checkout that you do.

You will also be surprised about some people's concept of what is important and what is not. I once checked out a pilot from another school who had flown the aircraft very well, but had struggled to perform a weight and balance calculation. He wanted to take two friends with him on a flight the following week, so I worked through a calculation with him based on a full fuel load, as an example. When we entered the figures on the graph it was within the maximum weight, but outside the centre of gravity envelope. As we looked at this, he said that he thought it didn't matter where the C of G position was as long as it was within the weight limit – or that's what one of his flying friends at his previous flying school had told him. In a diplomatic way, I categorically told him that it did matter where the C of G position was (in fact it mattered a lot) and in order for his proposed flight to go ahead he would need to take less fuel. We worked through another calculation with less fuel, which gave a result well within the envelope, and again I emphasized the importance of being within both weight and C of G limitations for a flight to go ahead safely, and legally.

An important point to remember on checkouts is that no matter how experienced, or inexperienced, the pilot being checked out is, always be prepared for the unexpected. When you fly with a student you are permanently on your guard for them doing strange things, but somehow on a checkout, when the person does already hold a licence, it is easy to subconsciously expect that they will know what they are doing. Whilst this is largely the case, you must never sit back and just let them get on with it.

I once had to check out a man who was new to the flying school, but who had several hundred hours on the aircraft type that we operated. He was extremely thorough and efficient in his pre-flight checks and gave the impression of being in total control of the situation. Once airborne his general handling of the aircraft was excellent, and when returning for some circuits he set up a beautifully trimmed base leg and final with minimal effort. Having been thoroughly impressed by the man's obvious abilities I was relaxed and comfortable in anticipation of a perfectly greased touchdown. I was therefore startled, to say the least, when during the flare he shoved the stick forward to the extent that we bounced heavily on the nosewheel, and pleasant thoughts about my forthcoming lunch were replaced, in a split second, by grabbing the controls and initiating a go-around to prevent the forthcoming crash!

Whatever the person's level of ability, always ensure that they reach the standard you require before their checkout is said to be complete, and if you are not satisfied that they have met this standard by the end of your session, tell them they will have to come back for some more. This can sometimes cause awkwardness, especially if the person thinks their flying was perfectly good, but ultimately you are the instructor and it is entirely your decision, not theirs. When a pilot has reached a standard that you are happy with it is often a good idea, if time and circumstances permit, to encourage them to go off on their own, even it is just for one solo circuit. Sometimes if the person has not flown for a while, and especially if they have not flown solo for a while, they will feel slightly anxious about their first flight on their own, so by flying on their own straight away and under the supervision of an instructor they will restore their confidence in their own abilities.

On this point, you may unfortunately find that on occasion, a pilot whom you have checked out will go flying on their own and will make some sort of mistake (at which point you will hear the immortal words from your fellow instructors, echoing down the corridor, 'Who checked him out?'). It is impossible for you to control another pilot's actions once they are on their own and you should not feel compelled to take responsibility for any mistakes that they make. You can only make a judgement from their performance during their flight with you, and if everything was satisfactory then the checkout is complete. If you have acted professionally, ensuring that a thorough checkout has been completed and all the relevant paperwork is in order then your work is done – and what the pilot subsequently chooses to do is their own responsibility, not yours.

CHAPTER 7
LICENSING RULES
AND REGULATIONS

When you are at work it is inevitable that you will be asked questions on licensing matters from time to time, such as how to go about renewing a lapsed IMC rating or the procedure for flying in the UK on the basis of a non-UK licence. Frequently people will telephone the flying school to ask these types of questions and often, if ops don't know the answer themselves, they will ask an instructor. Alternatively it may be that someone calls in to the flying school with a query and you just happen to be there to speak to them. Either way, it is a good idea to be able to answer any questions that they may have so that it reflects well on the school, but also on you as an instructor. After all, the person may just be about to book some lessons in order to renew their licence and if you were friendly and knowledgeable when they talked to you, they are likely to ask if they can fly with you. If, on the other hand, they spoke to you and you didn't appear to know anything then they will probably make every effort to be booked in to fly with someone else!

As a licence holder yourself you will be able to answer all the basic questions easily, and as an instructor you will be familiar with the requirements for straightforward licence revalidations and renewals. Occasionally, however, someone will come up with a really obscure question or one that you have not encountered before, and to which you may not immediately know the answer. It is therefore important to be able to find the most up-to-date information on the subject, to enable you to answer any queries as swiftly, but above all, as accurately, as you can. There are three specific licensing matters that you are likely to be asked questions on: medical certificates, UK-issued licences and non-UK licences.

MEDICAL CERTIFICATES

Questions regarding medical certificates are usually easy to answer as there are only two types of medical certificate issued by AMEs in the UK relevant to JAR licences – Class One and Class Two – each consisting of various components such as the electrocardiogram and audiogram, and having individual validity periods for each specific component within the certificate. (*See* below for the NPPL.) The only variables to take into account are the certificate holder's age and the class of certificate held or applied for. The requirements do change from time to time, however, and it is worth regularly checking LASORS and JAR-FCL 3 (Medical) (*see* Useful Information) to keep abreast of any changes that may have occurred recently.

A more difficult question on the subject of medicals might be about a particular medical condition and whether this would affect or prevent someone from obtaining their desired class of medical certificate. In such a case, you should refer the person directly to the CAA Medical Division at Gatwick (*see* Useful Information) who would be able to provide them with a definitive answer. Where medical matters are concerned, each individual case will have its own unique set of circumstances and it is not even worth speculating on the probable answer that the CAA might give; questions such as these often come from people with ambitions of becoming a commercial pilot, so there is no point in trying to be helpful and making an educated guess if your guess subsequently turns out to be wrong.

In terms of the NPPL, the medical standard required is based on that necessary to gain DVLA 2 (professional driver) and DVLA 1 (private driver) licences. To fly solo, a person must be able to achieve the DVLA 2 medical standard. If a person can achieve the DVLA 1 standard but a medical condition exists to prevent the DVLA 2 standard being reached, the person must always fly with a safety pilot. Applicants for a NPPL have to sign their own declaration of fitness to fly, and this must be countersigned by their GP to confirm that there is no known reason that the required standard of medical fitness cannot be met. This statement is merely based on the person's medical history, however, as there is no requirement for the GP to actually carry out a medical examination for this purpose. Specific details regarding NPPL medical matters can be obtained from the Popular Flying Association (*see* Useful Information).

UK-ISSUED LICENCES

In your day-to-day job, you will primarily be dealing with people who hold, or are working towards obtaining, UK-issued licences. This term covers any licence issued in the UK, so applies to licences issued under the old national (or CAA) licensing system, those subsequently issued under the European (or JAR) licensing system, and the National Private Pilot's Licence which is managed mainly by the Popular Flying Association and is issued by the CAA. It also applies to both private and commercial licences, as the people who fly light aircraft at a flying school will invariably be a whole mixture of people, holding every possible level of pilot's licence.

With this in mind, it should be remembered that a rating is issued and maintained in line with the same requirements, regardless of whether it is attached to a PPL or an ATPL. For example, an airline captain who flies multi-engine jets might decide that they would like to hire one of your school's single-engine aircraft, and in order to do this they must hold a current Single-Engine Piston (SEP) Class Rating. They might therefore call

A SEP Rating can be included in a PPL, CPL or ATPL.

into the flying school and speak to you to find out what training and testing would be necessary for them to renew their SEP Rating accordingly.

The time you spend dealing with licensing rules and regulations in the flying school environment will mostly, however, be concerning the revalidation and renewal of ratings held within a Private Pilot's Licence, and it is firstly worth noting some points regarding UK-issued PPLs:

- A CAA PPL remains valid for the holder's lifetime.
- A JAR PPL remains valid for five years but will be re-issued upon receipt of the currently specified fee, as stated in the ANO 'Scheme of Charges' (*see* Useful Information).

Therefore, when talking about revalidations and renewals it is not the licence itself which is being revalidated or renewed but a particular rating held within that licence. To clarify these terms:

- A revalidation takes place prior to the date of expiry of the rating.
- A renewal takes place after the date of expiry of the rating.

What follows, then, are the requirements for the revalidation and renewal of ratings that are most frequently included in the licences of pilots who fly light aircraft, regardless of the level of licence that the pilot holds.

Single-Engine Piston

The Single-Pilot, Single-Engine Piston (or SEP) (Land) Class Rating is valid for twenty-four months from the date of passing the Skill Test for the initial issue of the rating. In order to exercise the privileges of a SEP Rating beyond this twenty-four-month period, the holder of the rating must either revalidate it or renew it. The exact requirements for the revalidation or renewal of a rating are subject to change, but currently the requirements are as follows:

a) Revalidation of SEP (Land) Class Rating, by experience
Within the second year of the two-year validity period, the applicant must have completed twelve hours of flight time in SEP aircraft, to include:

- twelve take-offs and twelve landings
- six hours as Pilot-in-Command
- a training flight of at least one hour's duration, with an instructor. It must be entered as 'dual' flight time in the applicant's logbook, and the instructor must sign the logbook accordingly.

The training flight has its own list of requirements to be fulfilled and these are currently detailed on AIC 127/1999 (White 378) (*see* Useful Information). This training flight may be replaced by any Licensing Proficiency Check (LPC) or Skill Test for a Class, Type, Instrument or IMC Rating with an Examiner, that the pilot has undertaken within the same time period (i.e. the second year of the two-year validity period). It is worth noting that any flying experience gained within the first year of the two-year validity period will not count towards a SEP Rating revalidation by experience.

Once all the requirements have been met to revalidate a SEP Rating by experience, the applicant can produce their logbook evidence to an Examiner at any time within the three months prior to the date that it expires, and their SEP Rating will be revalidated from its existing expiry date without forfeiting any of its existing validity period. If signed prior to this final three months, the new validity period will commence from the date of signing, not the date of expiry, and will therefore forfeit the time remaining on the existing validity period. When satisfied that all the revalidation requirements have been fulfilled, the Examiner will sign the Certificate of Revalidation page in the applicant's licence. No fee is payable to the CAA.

b) Revalidation of SEP (Land) Class Rating, by LPC
As an alternative to revalidating a SEP Rating by experience, the applicant can elect to undertake an LPC for the purpose with a Flight Examiner. Details of the content of the LPC are listed in JAR-FCL 1.240, Appendices 1 and 3 (*see* Useful Information). If this is completed in the three months prior to the expiry date of their SEP Rating then the applicant will not forfeit any of the validity period of their existing rating, as the new rating expiry date will

be calculated from the existing rating expiry date. If the LPC is completed earlier than within this final three months, however, the new expiry date will be calculated from the date of the LPC and not the expiry date of the rating, thereby losing the remaining validity period of the rating. Upon successful completion of the LPC, the Examiner will sign the Certificate of Revalidation page in the applicant's licence. No fee is payable to the CAA.

c) Renewal of SEP (Land) Class Rating, if expired by a period not exceeding five years

No mandatory additional training is specified by the CAA but applicants should complete training at their own discretion, sufficient to pass a Skill Test with a Flight Examiner. Details of the content of the Skill Test are listed in JAR-FCL 1.240, Appendices 1 and 3. The applicant must also pass an oral theoretical knowledge examination conducted by the Examiner as part of the Skill Test. Once both these components have been successfully passed, the Examiner will sign the Certificate of Revalidation page in the applicant's licence. No fee is payable to the CAA.

d) Renewal of SEP (Land) Class Rating, if expired by a period exceeding five years

Again, no mandatory additional training is specified by the CAA but the applicant must be able to pass a Skill Test with a Flight Examiner in accordance with JAR-FCL 1.240, Appendices 1 and 3. The applicant must also pass an oral theoretical knowledge examination conducted by the Examiner as part of the Skill Test. Once both these components have been successfully passed, the appropriate fee should be sent to the CAA Personnel Licensing Department (*see* Useful Information), as stated in the current ANO 'Scheme of Charges'. No licence entry should be made by the Examiner as this endorsement will be made directly by the CAA.

Multi-Engine Piston

The Single-Pilot, Multi-Engine Piston (or MEP) (Land) Class Rating is valid for twelve months from the date of issue and can currently be revalidated or renewed as follows:

a) Revalidation of MEP (Land) Class Rating

The applicant must complete an LPC with a Flight Examiner within the three months preceding the expiry date of the rating. Details of the content of the LPC are listed in JAR-FCL 1.240, Appendices 1 and 3. Additionally, the applicant must have also completed at least ten route sectors in MEP aircraft within the validity period of the rating, a route sector being defined as a flight comprising take-off, cruise of not less than fifteen minutes, arrival, approach and landing. This experience requirement may be substituted by a single route sector flown with an Examiner, however, and this can be completed as part of the LPC.

Provided that the LPC is flown within the stated three-month period, the new rating validity period will commence from the expiry date of the existing rating. If the LPC is completed prior to this final three months, the new rating validity period will commence from the date of LPC, not the expiry date of the rating, and will thereby forfeit the remaining validity period of the rating. The applicant should provide the Examiner with evidence that all the revalidation requirements have been met and, if satisfied, the Examiner will then sign the Certificate of Revalidation page in the applicant's licence. No fee is payable to the CAA.

b) Renewal of MEP (Land) Class Rating, if expired by a period not exceeding five years
No mandatory additional training is specified by the CAA but applicants should complete training at their own discretion, sufficient to pass an LPC with a Flight Examiner in accordance with JAR-FCL 1.240, Appendices 1 and 3. Upon successful completion of the LPC, the Examiner will sign the Certificate of Revalidation page in the applicant's licence. No fee is payable to the CAA.

c) Renewal of MEP (Land) Class Rating, if expired by a period exceeding five years
The applicant must complete type technical training and obtain a pass in the ground examination, in accordance with the requirements of the Type Rating Training Organization (TRTO) or Flight Training Organization (FTO), as applicable. The applicant must also complete flying or simulator refresher training at the discretion of the Head of Training at the TRTO or FTO. The applicant must then pass an LPC with a Flight Examiner, in accordance with JAR-FCL 1.240, Appendices 1 and 3. Once all these components have been successfully completed, the appropriate fee should be sent to the CAA Personnel Licensing Department, as stated in the current ANO 'Scheme of Charges'. No licence entry should be made by the Examiner as this endorsement will be made directly by the CAA.

IMC Rating
The Instrument Meteorological Conditions (or IMC) Rating is valid for a period of twenty-five months from the date that the initial IMC Rating Flight Test was successfully passed. In order to exercise the privileges of the rating beyond this date, it must currently be revalidated or renewed as follows:

a) Revalidation of IMC Rating
The applicant must complete a revalidation Flight Test with a Flight Examiner. Details of the content of the Flight Test are listed in LASORS, Section E3, Appendix B. The applicant must also provide logbook evidence that within the validity period of their rating, they have successfully completed a let-down and approach to DH/MDH, a go-around and a

missed approach procedure, to the satisfaction of an instructor qualified to give instrument-flying instruction. This must have used a different type of aid from that used during the test. Alternatively, the applicant may carry out two approach procedures, using different aids, during the test.

b)Renewal of IMC Rating, if expired by a period not exceeding five years
Where an applicant wishes to renew an IMC Rating that has expired by a period not exceeding five years, they must satisfy the requirements as per an IMC Rating revalidation at (a), above.

c)Renewal of IMC Rating, if expired by a period exceeding five years but less than ten years
The applicant must undertake dual flight instruction with an instructor qualified to give instrument instruction and in a suitably equipped aircraft, covering the entire content of the IMC Rating course. The structure and extent of instruction given is at the discretion of the CFI. The applicant must then pass the initial IMC Rating Flight Test with a Flight Examiner.

d)Renewal of IMC Rating, if expired by a period exceeding ten years
Where an applicant wishes to renew an IMC Rating that has expired by a period exceeding ten years, they must satisfy the requirements as per an IMC Rating renewal at (c), above. They must also pass the IMC ground examination.

It cannot be emphasized enough that where the revalidation of any rating is concerned, an applicant must ensure that they produce the necessary evidence and documents to an Examiner prior to the date of expiry of the rating. Irrespective of the fact that all the requirements for a revalidation may have indeed been satisfied, if the expiry date of the rating has already passed when it is presented then that rating is deemed to have lapsed. This means that a revalidation would no longer apply and therefore a renewal would become necessary instead.

Night Qualification
Once obtained, this qualification does not expire and hence there are no requirements for its revalidation or renewal. In practice, of course, a flying school is unlikely to allow a pilot to hire one of their aircraft for a night flight if their last night flight was a significant length of time ago, despite the fact that it would be perfectly legal to do so. Each specific flying school will have their own rules regarding night currency, and details of these will be stated in their Flying Order Book. The only requirement stipulated by the CAA is that if a pilot wishes to carry passengers at night, one of their three take-offs and landings undertaken as part of the ninety-day rule (discussed earlier) must have been at night.

Most queries concern the SEP Rating, IMC Rating and night qualification.

Differences and Familiarization Training

In order to fly a different type or variant of aircraft within the same Class Rating, or another variant within the same Type Rating, a pilot must undertake Differences Training or Familiarization Training. To define these terms:

- Differences Training requires both theoretical knowledge instruction and training on the aircraft, or appropriate training device.
- Familiarization Training requires the acquisition of additional knowledge relevant to the new type or variant, which can be achieved by self-study, with the assistance of another pilot already experienced on type, or from an instructor. Familiarization Training is only sufficient where Differences Training is not required.

If a pilot wishes to fly a different type, or variant of a type, which falls within the Single-Pilot SEP Class Rating, Single-Pilot MEP Class Rating, or Single-Pilot Type Rating that they hold, then Differences Training is required. This training is specifically required to encompass particular 'complex' features with which the new type or variant may be equipped, and these features are:

- Variable Pitch (VP) propeller(s)
- Retractable undercarriage
- Turbocharged or supercharged engine(s)
- Cabin pressurization
- Tailwheel

Where a pilot has completed Differences Training on an aircraft within a Single-Pilot MEP Class Rating or Single-Pilot Type Rating, they would not be required to undertake equivalent Differences Training on an aircraft within a Single-Pilot SEP Class Rating. If, however, a pilot has completed Differences Training on an aircraft within a Single-Pilot SEP Class Rating, then this would not count towards the requirement for Differences Training on an aircraft within a Single-Pilot MEP Class Rating or Single-Pilot Type Rating.

It would be impossible to produce a syllabus of training to cover every individual situation, and therefore the training to be undertaken is largely left to the judgement of the instructor. The primary source of reference for this training should be the aircraft Flight Manual or, where no Flight Manual is available, the Pilot's Operating Handbook or Pilot's Notes, and when considering what to include in the training instructors must carefully consider the experience of the student in question. Details regarding the content of the instruction to be provided are stated in LASORS and this should be consulted for guidance in every individual case.

The National Private Pilot's Licence

The NPPL can be issued for three classes of flying machine: 'Simple Single-Engine Aeroplane' (or SSEA), 'Self-Launching Motor Glider' (or SLMG), or 'Microlight and Powered Parachute'. As most flying schools are only equipped with single-engine piston aircraft for flight training, however, you are likely only to be dealing with training towards the NPPL (SSEA).

The NPPL (SSEA) can only be issued with a SSEA Class Rating. No additional ratings can be added to an NPPL. The licence itself does not expire, and an SSEA Rating within an NPPL does not have a finite validity period or expiry date as such. It is instead validated by means of a continuous experience process, or by means of a NPPL General Skill Test (GST). In order to exercise the privileges of an SSEA Rating contained within an NPPL, therefore, the holder must currently satisfy the following requirements:

- Within the twelve-month period preceding the date of a flight, the holder must have completed six hours of flight time including not less than four hours as pilot-in-command, and within the twenty-four month period preceding the date of a flight must have completed an instructional flight of at least one hour's duration, or
- Within the twelve-month period preceding the date of a flight, the holder must have undertaken and passed an NPPL GST with an Examiner.

In the case of a GST being taken, upon successful completion of the test the Examiner will sign and enter the date of test on the Certificate of Revalidation page of the NPPL. No expiry date will be shown, however, as the validity may in the future be maintained by the continuous experience process and thus will not have 'expired' after any particular date. Where the holder of a SSEA Rating has not satisfied the above requirements for their rating to be considered valid, the rating is deemed to have lapsed. The holder will therefore need to renew their rating according to the following current requirements:

a) Renewal of SSEA Class Rating, if expired by a period not exceeding five years
The applicant will be required to undertake and pass an NPPL GST, and hold a valid NPPL medical certificate.

b) Renewal of SSEA Class Rating, if expired by a period exceeding five years but less than ten years
The applicant will be required to undergo a course of training at the discretion of a flying instructor in order to undertake and pass both the NPPL Navigation Skill Test (NST) and GST. The applicant must also hold a valid NPPL medical certificate.

c) Renewal of SSEA Class Rating, if expired by a period exceeding ten years
The applicant will be required to undergo a course of training at the discretion of a flying instructor, which must include:

- two hours of stall awareness and spin avoidance training,
- four hours of solo general handling exercises, and
- four hours of solo cross-country flying, including the NPPL qualifying cross-country flight.

They must undertake and pass the NPPL NST and GST, and hold a valid NPPL medical certificate. In addition, the applicant must pass all the JAR-FCL PPL (A) theoretical knowledge examinations.

Credit of Microlight Experience Towards an NPPL (SSEA)

Since the introduction of the NPPL, many microlight pilots have elected to use their microlight experience towards the grant of an NPPL (SSEA), and you may therefore find yourself being asked about this when you are at work.

Where the holder of a valid NPPL (Microlight and Powered Parachute) without restrictions wishes to obtain an NPPL (SSEA), they must be able to produce logbook evidence of currency on microlight aircraft and undergo a course of training on SSEA aircraft at the discretion of a flying instructor, which must include:

- not less than one hour of dual instrument appreciation,
- two hours of stall awareness and spin avoidance training,
- Differences Training for pilots whose microlight experience has been gained solely on flexwing machines, and
- in total, not less than the thirty-two hours minimum flight time required for the NPPL (SSEA), which may be a combination of both microlight and SSEA experience.

They must undertake and pass the NPPL (SSEA) NST and GST, and hold a valid NPPL medical certificate or JAR-FCL Class One or Class Two medical certificate. In addition, the applicant must pass all the JAR-FCL PPL (A) theoretical knowledge examinations.

Further details regarding NPPL matters are contained within LASORS or available from the Popular Flying Association, although enquiries on each of the specific licences should be directed to the following bodies:

- For NPPL (SSEA): contact the Aircraft Owners and Pilots Association (AOPA).
- For NPPL (SLMG): contact the British Gliding Association (BGA).
- For NPPL (Microlight and Powered Parachute): contact the British Microlight Aircraft Association (BMAA).

(Contact details for all these bodies are listed in the Useful Information.)

Hours Flown Abroad

An area in which questions are often asked is on the subject of hours flown whilst abroad. People who hold licences or are training towards them will frequently take the opportunity to go flying whilst they are abroad, and consequently you will often be asked whether these hours will count towards the pilot's total logged hours and, more specifically, if they will count towards a particular revalidation or renewal (such as the twelve-hour requirement for a SEP Rating revalidation). Whether the CAA will recognize a pilot's flying hours logged whilst abroad is dependent on many factors, including details of the specific aircraft flown, the flying school flown from and the particular licence held by the instructor. There are an almost infinite number of variables when considering a flight or flights undertaken in any aircraft, with any instructor, anywhere in the world, and it would therefore be impossible to list all such possibilities, in every combination, in a document. If faced with a query of this nature, the CAA should be contacted as each case will need to be judged according to its own unique circumstances.

NON-UK LICENCES

There are likely to be occasions when people with non-UK licences will enquire about hiring aircraft from your flying school. There will be a wide variety of purposes for these pilots wishing to fly in the UK, such as if they are over here on holiday or on business, or if they have moved over here permanently, and the circumstances surrounding each individual case will entirely dictate the advice you should give them. By far the most straightforward situation is when the holder of a non-UK licence wants to go flying in the UK, purely for the experience, and they can achieve this very easily just by going up with an instructor. There would be no paperwork involved on the licensing side because the instructor would be pilot-in-command and the flight would simply be logged as a dual flight, the same as any other dual flight. If the holder of a non-UK licence wants to hire the aircraft and fly themselves without an instructor, or in fact convert their own licence to a UK licence, however, then there are many more factors to consider.

Flying in the UK on the Privileges of a Non-UK Licence

In order to fly a UK-registered aircraft, a pilot must hold a licence that is 'rendered valid under the ANO'. Any JAA licence is deemed to be valid under the ANO, where the licence is issued in accordance with the licensing and medical requirements of JAR-FCL by a full JAA Member State, and unless in a particular case the CAA decides otherwise. A licence issued by any other ICAO Contracting State is also deemed to be valid under the ANO for the purposes of flying a UK-registered aircraft, providing that the licence and medical certificate are valid in accordance with the rules and laws of the issuing state, and unless in a particular case the CAA decides otherwise. However, the holder of such a licence is not entitled to:

- act as a member of the flight crew for the purpose of public transport or aerial work,
- receive remuneration for acting as a member of the flight crew,
- act as the pilot of any aircraft flying in controlled airspace in circumstances requiring compliance with Instrument Flight Rules,
- give any instruction in flying.

Therefore, if you have an enquiry from a pilot who holds a licence fulfilling the above criteria, and the flying they wish to undertake does not include any of the above points, one to four, then in principle they are able to fly one of your school's aircraft. The complications only arise when formulating a plan for their checkout, because the pilot's whole experience of flying is likely to be different from that existing in the UK. Everything from R/T procedures to the aeronautical charts in use may be totally unfamiliar to them, so a very detailed and thorough checkout would be necessary, but the actual content and length of such a checkout would be entirely at the discretion of your flying school.

Converting a Non-UK Licence to a UK Licence

Where a pilot wishes to be granted a UK licence on the basis of their non-UK licence, specific details about their non-UK licence will need to be considered. As variations exist between each individual country's flight-training syllabus, ground-examination syllabus and medical requirements (even between JAA Member States), an assessment and judgement will often need to be made in each individual case. Much information on the subject is contained in LASORS, so this document should be consulted initially, but it is likely that the pilot will need to contact the CAA Personnel Licensing Department in order to obtain a definitive answer. Once the CAA have made an assessment they will issue a list of any training requirements to be undertaken by the pilot, which could range from very little, to virtually the same requirements as for someone with no previous experience at all. It will include details of any flight and ground training to be undertaken, plus any ground examinations and flight tests which must be passed, providing you as the instructor with all the information that you need to formulate a suitable course of training for them.

CONCLUSION

When someone has come to you with a question on licensing matters and you have provided them with an answer, it is always a good idea to give them a hard copy of the information you have provided, or at least to tell them where to obtain it for themselves. This means that they can study the information at their leisure, absorb it thoroughly, and be able to refer back to it where necessary. It will also enable them to find their own answers to any other questions they may think of, although you should make it very clear to them to always ensure they are referring to the latest, and therefore most accurate, information available.

As mentioned throughout this section, the exact requirements for the revalidation and renewal of specific ratings held within a licence are constantly evolving and are therefore subject to change at any time. The authoritative point of reference for information on these, and other, requirements is the document LASORS which is published annually by the

CAA, and all the details in this book are stated according to LASORS 2005. Any changes that occur in the interim between publications should be promulgated by the CAA via AICs or as direct amendments to LASORS, and both LASORS and all the current AICs are available from the CAA website.

There are more unusual ratings that you may come across at your flying school which are not mentioned in this chapter, such as a Single-Pilot Type Rating for an aircraft that is not covered by the Single-Engine Piston or Multi-Engine Piston Class Rating, and the details for each one will be stated in LASORS. If your specific query does not appear to be explained in LASORS, then you should contact the CAA Personnel Licensing Department directly for an authoritative answer.

USEFUL INFORMATION

Terminal Aerodrome Forecasts (TAFs)

Civilian Airfields		Military Airfields	
validity period (Z)	time of issue (Z)	validity period (Z)	time of issue (Z)
0413	0330	0312	0230
0716	0630	0615	0530
1019	0930	0918	0830
1322	1230	1221	1130
1601	1530	1500	1430
1904	1830	1803	1730
2207	2130	2106	2030
0110	0030	0009	2330

NB: All times are ZULU (Greenwich Mean Time), in terms of both the issue time and any times stated within the forecast, so bear this in mind during the British Summer Time (BST) months when local time in the UK is one hour ahead.

The time of issue is the time at which the TAF is usually available from the Met Office (on the website or by telephone), or from other sources of aviation weather information. As shown above, this should be thirty minutes prior to the commencement of the validity period of the forecast, although in practice the information is sometimes not available until a while later.

USEFUL ADDRESSES

Met Office
FitzRoy Road
Exeter
Devon
EX1 3PB

Tel: 0870 900 0100
Fax: 0870 900 5050
Email: enquiries@metoffice.gov.uk
Website: www.metoffice.com

Aeronautical Information Service
National Air Traffic Services Ltd
Control Tower Building
London Heathrow Airport
Hounslow
Middlesex
TW6 1JJ

Tel: UK AIP section 020 8745 3456
       NOTAM and PIB information 020 8745 3450/3451
       General Enquiries 020 8745 3464
Email: ais.supervisor@nats.co.uk
Website: www.ais.org.uk

Civil Aviation Authority – Personnel Licensing Department (PLD)
Safety Regulation Group
Aviation House (GE)
Gatwick Airport South
West Sussex
RH6 0YR

Tel: 01293 573700
Fax: 01293 573996
Email: fclweb@srg.caa.co.uk
Website: www.caa.co.uk

Civil Aviation Authority (Medical Centre)
Safety Regulation Group
Aviation House (GE)
Gatwick Airport South
West Sussex
RH6 0YR

Tel: 01293 573700
Fax: 01293 573995
Email: medicalweb@srg.caa.co.uk
Website: www.caa.co.uk

Joint Aviation Authorities
Saturnusstraat 8–10
PO Box 3000
2130 KA Hoofddorp
The Netherlands

Fax: (31) (0) 23 - 5621714
Website: www.jaa.nl

Popular Flying Association (PFA) Ltd
Turweston Aerodrome
Brackley
Northamptonshire
NN13 5YD

Tel: 01280 846786
Fax: 01280 846780
Email: office@pfa.org.uk
Website: www.pfa.org.uk

Aircraft Owners and Pilots Association (AOPA)
50A Cambridge Street
London
SW1V 4QQ

Tel: 020 7834 5631
Fax: 020 7834 2623
Email: info@aopa.co.uk
Website: www.aopa.co.uk

British Gliding Association (BGA)
Kimberley House
Vaughan Way
Leicester
LE1 4SE

Tel: 0116 253 1051
Fax: 0116 251 5939
Email: bga@gliding.co.uk
Website: www.gliding.co.uk

British Microlight Aircraft Association (BMAA)
Deddington
Banbury
Oxfordshire
OX15 0TT

Tel: 01869 338888
Fax: 01869 337116
Website: www.bmaa.org

FORMS FOR YOUR FILE

Shown below are some examples of the forms, certificates and reference material that could be included in your file, as discussed in Chapter Two. As this section states, many flying schools have a whole array of their own forms and documents which you will be asked to use, but other schools may only have certain forms of their own (such as a Qualifying Cross-Country certificate), in which case you may decide to draw up some of the other forms yourself (such as a weight and balance sheet) to make your working life easier.

The sheets below are provided to offer suggestions on how to lay out the information, and can be used as the basis for your own forms, if you wish. Much of the information contained within them is specific to a particular aircraft or airfield, however: they should not be used directly, in their current format, but amended to include the data relevant to your particular aircraft, airfield and circumstances.

Once again it should be noted that changes do frequently occur, so the latest aeronautical information should always be sought to ensure that the correct details are being used.

The material shown is not for planning purposes.

Local Airfield Locator Details

Airfield	Ident	Freq	Range
Blackpool:	BPL	420	15nm
Caernarfon:	CAE	320	15nm
Hawarden:	HAW	340	25nm
Liverpool:	LPL	349.5	25nm
Manchester:	MCH	428	15nm
Man Barton:	BAE	325	10nm
Man Woodford:	WFD	380	15nm
Shobdon:	SH	426	20nm
Sleap:	SLP	382	10nm
Tatenhill:	TNL	327	10nm
Welshpool:	WPL	323	10nm
Wolverhampton:	WBA	356	25nm

Solo Circuit Briefing Certificate

ITEMS CHECKED AND DISCUSSED PRE-FLIGHT:

    1. FLYING SCHOOL RULES AND FLYING REGULATIONS
        * Flying Order Book read and signed

    2. AEROPLANE
        * Fuel and oil state
        * Ignition systems
        * Use of carburettor heat
        * Mixture controls

    3. NORMAL PROCEDURES
        * Taxy
        * R/T
        * Circuit height / direction for all runways
        * Apron and parking

    4. EMERGENCY PROCEDURES:
        * Missed approach procedure
        * Abandoned take off
        * Brake failure
        * EFATO
        * Action in event of fire, on ground or in air:
                –engine
                –cabin
                –electrical
        * Flap failure
        * Electrical failure
        * Radio failure

I CERTIFY THAT I HAVE BEEN FULLY BRIEFED FOR THE ABOVE EXERCISE.

_____   _____

STUDENT NAME/SIGNATURE   DATE/TIME

_____   _____

INSTRUCTOR NAME/SIGNATURE   DATE/TIME

Qualifying Cross-Country Certificate

This is to certify that _____ Student Pilot,

pilot of aircraft_____ type and registration,

was authorised to depart _____ airfield

at _____ time on _____ date,

for the purpose of their qualifying cross-country, in accordance with JAR-FCL 1 Subpart C.

Routing: _____

_____

Alternates: _____

_____

FI signature: _____

Name & Licence No: _____

FIRST INTERMEDIATE AIRFIELD

This is to certify that the above named pilot landed

at _____ airfield

at _____ time on _____ date,

Their standard of airmanship was

_____

Their standard of landing was

_____

To the best of my knowledge the pilot was alone, and unaccompanied by any other aircraft.

FI or ATC signature: _____

Name & Licence No: _____

SECOND INTERMEDIATE AIRFIELD

This is to certify that the above named pilot landed

at _____ airfield

at _____ time on _____ date,

Their standard of airmanship was.

_____

Their standard of landing was

_____

To the best of my knowledge the pilot was alone, and unaccompanied by any other aircraft.

FI or ATC signature: _____

Name & Licence No: _____

The Qualifying Cross-Country detailed above was carried out to my satisfaction, and in accordance with the requirements of JAR-FCL.

CFI signature: _____

Name & Licence No: _____

NOTE TO PILOT: This form must be completed at each airfield you land at. Any problems or unscheduled landings should be reported to your supervising instructor as soon as possible.

Instructor contact number/s: _____

_____

_____

Solo Navigation Briefing Certificate

AGREED ROUTE: _____

_____

_____

_____

AIRFIELD DETAILS (inc. alternates):

Name: _____   Name: _____

Last landing time (local): _____   Last landing time (local): _____

Tel number: _____   Tel number: _____

ETA (local): _____   ETA (local): _____

Name: _____   Name: _____

Last landing time (local): _____   Last landing time (local): _____

Tel number: _____   Tel number: _____

ETA (local): _____   ETA (local): _____

ITEMS CHECKED AND DISCUSSED PRE-FLIGHT:

1. Weather   – Latest TAFs, METARs (or observations), 214, 215.

2. Route   – Need for, and method for maintaining, flight in VMC.
        – Planned altitude, MSA, altimeter setting procedures.
        – Procedures approaching/inside controlled airspace, ATZ,
          MATZ, Danger/Prohibited/Restricted Areas.
        – Current NOTAMs, Navigational warnings, Royal Flights.

3.Airfields   – PPR.
               – Position reporting, joining procedure for runway in use.
               – Parking, refuelling, booking in and out.

4.Radio   – Use of r/t and transponder for normal procedures.
               – Urgency and emergency procedures: VHF/DF, Pan,
                 Mayday.

5.Aircraft   – Fuel and oil state (endurance noted), aircraft
                serviceability.
               – Weight and balance, performance calculated for all
                runways.

ABNORMAL AND EMERGENCY PROCEDURES

Intrusion into controlled airspace, radio failure, lost, deteriorating weather, diversion, low fuel state, unscheduled landing, aircraft emergency.

I CERTIFY THAT I HAVE BEEN FULLY BRIEFED FOR THE ABOVE EXERCISE.

STUDENT NAME/SIGNATURE: _____

DATE/TIME: _____

INSTRUCTOR NAME/SIGNATURE: _____

DATE/TIME: _____

(Ops telephone number, Instructor telephone number)

_____

_____

Take-Off and Landing Factors

TAKE-OFF

Condition	Increase in take-off distance to height 50ft	Factor
10% increase in weight	20%	1.20
Increase of 1000ft in airfield altitude	10%	1.10
Increase of 10°c in temperature	10%	1.10
Dry grass -– up to 20cm (firm soil)	20%	1.20
Wet grass – up to 20cm (firm soil)	30%	1.30
2% uphill slope*	10%	1.10
Tailwind component of 10% of lift off speed	20%	1.20
Soft ground or snow*	25% or more	1.25+

*Effect on ground run/roll will be proportionally greater.

LANDING

Condition	Increase in landing distance from height 50ft	Factor
10% increase in weight	10%	1.10
Increase of 1000ft in airfield altitude	5%	1.05
Increase of 10°c in temerature	5%	1.05
Wet paved runway	15%	1.15
Dry grass – up to 20cm (firm soil)	15%	1.15
Wet grass – up to 20cm (firm soil)	35%	1.35
2% downhill slope*	10%	1.10
Tailwind component of 10% of landing speed	20%	1.20
Snow	25% or more	1.25+

*Effect on ground run/roll will be proportionally greater.

NOTE 1: After the above factors are applied, it is recommended to apply the public transport safety factors of 1.33 for take-off and 1.43 for landing.

NOTE 2: Any deviation from normal operating techniques is likely to increase the above distances.

NOTE 3: Very short grass may increase distances by up to 60% (1.60) as the surface may be slippery.

Local Area Radio Navigation Aids

Facility	Ident	Frequency	Range
Gamston VOR/DME	GAM	112.80Mhz	80nm
Isle of Man VOR/DME	IOM	112.20Mhz	60nm
Lichfield NDB	LIC	545.0kHz	50nm
Manchester VOR/DME	MCT	113.55MHz	90nm
Pole Hill VOR/DME	POL	112.10Mhz	115nm*
Shawbury VOR/DME	SWB	116.80Mhz	50nm
Trent VOR/DME	TNT	115.70Mhz	80nm
Wallasey VOR/DME	WAL	114.10Mhz	120nm
Whitegate NDB	WHI	368.5kHz	25nm

*Due to terrain, coverage at low level is reduced in sector RDL 284°–339°.

INDEX